ISSUES THAT CONCERN YOU

Teen Driving

Linda Aksomitis, *Book Editor*

GREENHAVEN PRESS
A part of Gale, Cengage Learning

GALE
CENGAGE Learning™

Detroit • New York • San Francisco • New Haven, Conn • Waterville, Maine • London

Christine Nasso, *Publisher*
Elizabeth Des Chenes, *Managing Editor*

LIBRARY OF CONGRESS CATALOGING-IN-PUBLICATION DATA

Teen driving / Linda Aksomitis, book editor.
p. cm. — (Issues that concern you)
Includes bibliographical references and index.
ISBN-13: 978-0-7377-4187-2 (hardcover)
1. Teenage automobile drivers. 2. Traffic safety—United States. I. Aksomitis, Linda.
HE5620.J8T4375 2008
363.12'52—dc22

2008021499

Printed in the United States of America
1 2 3 4 5 6 7 12 11 10 09 08

CONTENTS

In the case of *Robertson v. the Department of Public Works*, Justice Tolman of the Washington State Supreme Court stated that:

> Complete freedom of the highways is so old and well established a blessing that we have forgotten the days of the Robber Barons and toll roads, and yet, under an act like this [regarding a lack of jurisdiction in a case on driving without a license], arbitrarily administered, the highways may be completely monopolized; if, through lack of interest, the people submit, then they may look to see the most sacred of their liberties taken from them one by one, by more or less rapid encroachment.

The question remains, though: Is driving a right or a privilege? Nina A. of Byron Center, Michigan, published an article on teenink.com describing the day she decided it was indeed a privilege. While driving her little blue Geo Tracker early one morning, struggling to stay awake, she ran a red light and caused an accident. She wrote, "Nothing is more important than having enough sleep to drive safely and keep myself and others safe (and possibly even alive). These are all reminders of just how big a privilege driving really is."

If driving were considered a right, instead of a privilege, should anyone be able to just hop into a vehicle—car, truck, tractor trailer—and hit the interstate? What of learning the traffic laws first and passing a driver's license test? Should people have to study driving laws in advance, or will they automatically figure out how it all works when they jump behind the wheel of a 4,000-pound car or an 80,000-pound 18-wheeler? What happens if they do not figure it out quickly enough? Somebody dies.

The only way to minimize the millions of injuries and deaths that occur each year on American highways is to help teen drivers make their generation safer than the previous generation. This can be done with safety regulations for drivers and their vehicles, good

Sitting near the intersection where their best friend was killed in a car accident, these high school juniors grieve by a cross erected as a memorial to the dead girl.

training programs, and requiring practical experience behind the wheel of a vehicle before granting an unrestricted driver's license.

About a century has passed since the first American received a driver's license. The first affordable cars for people were not produced until Henry Ford's Model T in 1908, and there were not many cars around in those days. On August 1, 1910, North America's first driver licensing law went into effect in the state of New York. The law initially applied only to professional chauffeurs or any drivers who had passengers depending on their safe driving skills. In July 1913 the state of New Jersey became the first to require all drivers to pass a mandatory examination before receiving a license.

For modern teens, various aspects of their lifestyles are significantly changed when they become drivers. Simson L. Garfinkle in an article on *wired.com* says, "Driving is a privilege, not a right.

But it's a privilege that has become a virtual necessity. For many Americans, a driver's license is a also license to earn a living, see friends, go shopping, and get away from it all on the weekends."

As well as allowing drivers to legally operate motor vehicles, driver's licenses also serve as official documents to prove age and residency. Holders of a license may use it as photo identification to board an airplane. They may use a driver's license to purchase a state fishing or hunting license. They may even use a license as a form of identification to get a passport, which will allow them to visit other countries. With a driver's license so important in society, all drivers need to protect their right to have a license by knowing and following all the safe driving laws.

After a birth or baptismal certificate, a driver's license is usually a teen's first official document and is often considered the first step a teen makes toward the responsibilities of adulthood. Unlike a birth certificate, teens must earn a driver's license by exhibiting knowledge of driving and skill in handling a motor vehicle. Whether teens are fulfilling the requirements of a graduated licensing program or a teen-parent driving agreement, it is important for them to know their rights and responsibilities.

Before getting a driver's license, most teens seek out good programs to help them master their driving skills and attain the knowledge that will assist them in becoming safe, defensive drivers on the roads. However, earning a license is just a beginning, not an end. Once teens qualify for a regular driving license, miles of experience are still to be gained from traveling the nation's highways.

The following viewpoints provide young people with numerous perspectives on teen driving. Some topics are controversial, such as laws forbidding teens from using cell phones while driving or having global tracking units installed in their cars that will report their driving to parents. Other topics examine opposing sides of an issue, such as whether the legal driving age should be raised. In addition, the volume contains appendixes to help the reader understand the challenges faced by young drivers, as well as facts on driving various types of vehicles, both on and off the roads. The appendix "What You Should Do About Teen Driving" offers tips to students to help ensure that they have a safe trip every time they drive.

ONE

Raising the Teen Driving Age May Curb Teen Auto Fatalities

Sara Miller Llana

In the following viewpoint Sara Miller Llana explains that Massachusetts lawmakers are working to enact a law that will make teens wait one more year, until they are seventeen and a half, to take their driver's test.[1] She explores the controversy surrounding the issue, and suggests that perhaps Massachusetts should just enact a tougher graduated licensing system. The author says that Massachusetts already has a tough graduated licensing system in place, and that still three out of every ten sixteen-year-old drivers will be in a serious crash, according to the Massachusetts Registry of Motor Vehicles. The author suggests the issue of raising the teen driving age needs further exploration and discussion.

After a string of high-profile fatal car crashes involving teen drivers, Massachusetts lawmakers are working to add new speed bumps to getting a license.

Their aim: Make teens wait one more year—until they are 17-1/2—to take their driver's test. Other states are considering tougher restrictions on young drivers, from curfews to extra driv-

[1] In June 2006, the Massachusetts legislature passed a different, less controversial teen driving bill, which did *not* include raising the minimum driving age to seventeen and a half. The minimum driving age in the state remains sixteen and a half.

Sara Miller Llana, "Massachusetts Considers Raising the Driving Age to Curb Car Accidents Among Teens," *Christian Science Monitor*, March 29, 2006. Reproduced by permission from The Christian Science Monitor (www.csmonitor.com).

er's education, but the Bay State proposal still under consideration would make the wait here the longest in the country.

An Attempt to Curb Car Accidents Among Teens

Most experts agree that inexperience behind the wheel contributes to more accidents among teens. Although young drivers comprise only 7 percent of all drivers, 15 percent of drivers in fatal crashes are between ages 15 and 20.

Whether immaturity is a key factor is more questionable, experts say.

"Raising the licensing age will have a net benefit for the state of Massachusetts; maturity helps to lower your crash rate," says David Preusser, a Connecticut-based highway safety evaluator whose clients include the National Highway Traffic Safety

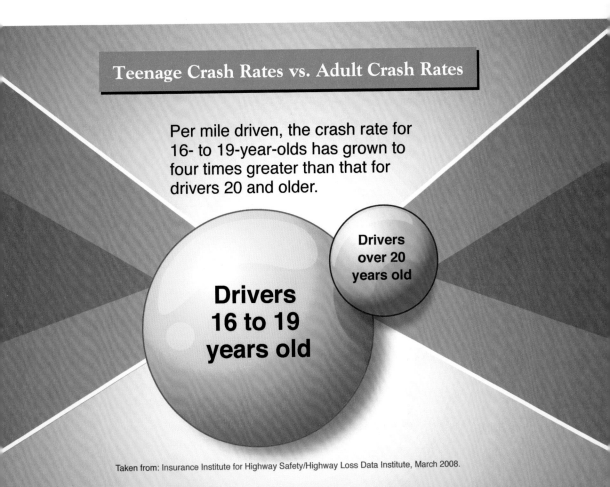

Teenage Crash Rates vs. Adult Crash Rates

Per mile driven, the crash rate for 16- to 19-year-olds has grown to four times greater than that for drivers 20 and older.

Drivers over 20 years old

Drivers 16 to 19 years old

Taken from: Insurance Institute for Highway Safety/Highway Loss Data Institute, March 2008.

Administration. But he says increased supervision in the first few months of licensure, during which his research shows accident rates spike, will better ensure safety. "If all you do is increase the age, [accidents during] those first few months of driving will just come at a later time."

In the past decade state legislatures have shied away from raising the driving age. Parents balk at additional months shuttling their children to extracurricular activities or work; a set of keys at age 16, meanwhile, is a celebrated rite of passage for teens.

Instead officials have toughened graduated licensing systems that phase teens in as drivers and provide more supervision.

Massachusetts already has a tough graduated system in place. Teens can get their learner permits at age 16, and do not get full licensure until age 18. Until then, they cannot drive between midnight and 5 a.m., and young, new drivers cannot carry passengers younger than 18, other than family members, unless supervised.

Still, three of every ten 16-year-old drivers will be in a serious crash, according to the Massachusetts Registry of Motor Vehicles.

Making Graduated Licensing Even Tougher

The debate here is an effort to make the graduated system even tougher. State Rep. Bradford Hill (R) of Ipswich, wants to increase driver's education courses and punishments for violators of junior operator laws. But he is against increasing the age requirements, which would make the state the strictest in the US behind New Jersey, where currently teens must wait until they turn 17 to drive unsupervised.

His constituents, he says, worry about sending their children to college without sufficient practice. He also warns of an unintended consequence: Currently only those under age 18 must take driver's education classes. Raising the age to 17-1/2 might be an incentive to bypass the course. "All they have to do is wait six months to get their licenses," he says.

That, say many, is counterproductive because increasing education requirements is what young drivers need most—on the road experience in a supervised, low-risk environment.

Some teenagers say they are upset by the proposal. "Just because [an accident] happened to one, it doesn't mean we are all like that," says Darren Hairston, 16, of Somerville, Mass. He got his permit in February, and is aiming for his license by August—which he says will help him get to his job.

Driving instructors have also criticized the measure, which would delay by six months the age at which teens could get their permits to 16-1/2, up from 16. Teen drivers are not less safe because they are young, says David Leung, who owns D & D Auto School in Boston. A third of his clients are teens, he says, and

A sherrif's deputy takes pictures of a fatal accident involving teenagers near Elizabethtown, Idaho. Many experts argue that the teen driving age should be raised to eighteen to help curtail teen driving fatalities.

many would benefit from more hours behind the wheel, practicing at large intersections and amidst heavy traffic.

The proposal would double the time they must drive with a learner's permit.

Research and Opinions on Teen Driving

Still, many say they welcome more research on whether maturity and judgment are underdeveloped among teen drivers, making them more likely to display risky behavior, such as speeding or passing other vehicles inappropriately.

Among 16- to 20-year-olds, the fatality rate in motor vehicle crashes was twice the rate for all ages in 2002. "There is some argument that if you can delay licensure, you have a more mature kid, but the whole discussion about it nationally is really premature," says Barbara Harsha, of the Governors Highway Safety Association. "It is not something that should be discouraged either."

Some teens agree with increasing the age restrictions. Regine Paulynice, 16, of Somerville says her mom won't let her start driving until she turns 18. "I think it's a good thing. Most kids do go crazy," she says. "They don't care what happens."

TWO

Raising the Teen Driving Age May Not Curb Teen Auto Fatalities

Raja Mishra

Raja Mishra wrote the following selection after the Massachusetts State Legislature abandoned an attempt to raise the minimum driving age to seventeen and a half, which would have been the highest in the United States. Mishra explains that the age increase was part of a bill that outlined various other changes to teen driving laws. While some new teen driving laws did go into effect on March 31, 2007, the driving age remained at sixteen and a half. Mishra points out that the new law did increase the amount of time teens had to spend driving with a parent or guardian, plus it greatly increased penalties for teens who speed, drag race, drive with passengers other than a parent or guardian during the first six months, or violate the rule against driving after midnight. Raja Mishra has worked as a reporter for the *Boston Globe*.

State lawmakers [in Massachusetts, on June 1, 2006] abandoned an effort to raise the state's minimum driving age to 17 1/2, which would have been the highest in the nation. A vote on the measure was abruptly postponed . . . on Beacon Hill after unexpectedly widespread opposition emerged.

"I don't think we are going to license at 17.5; I don't think that will happen," said state Representative Joseph F. Wagner, a Chicopee Democrat who is the bill's main author. Asked whether the age increase was dead, he replied, "That's fair to say."

Age Hike Proposal Part of Changes to Teen Driving Laws

The age hike was part of a larger proposal to overhaul teenage driving laws. The rest of the package—beefing up driver's education, increasing parent-supervised driving, and toughening penalties for violations of junior operator's licenses—remains intact. It [was] rescheduled for a House vote on June 14 [2006]. The other provisions in the bill [had] more widespread support, lawmakers said. . . .

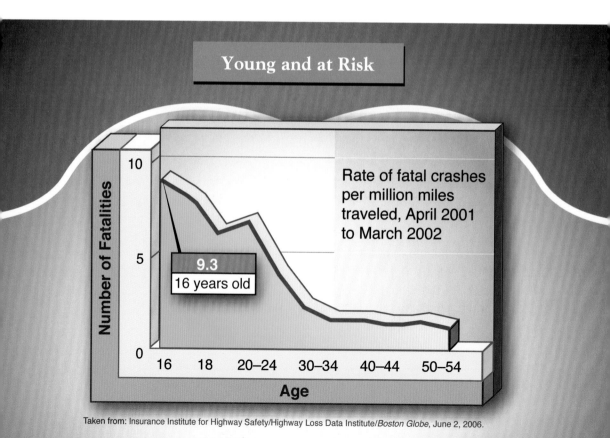

Young and at Risk

Rate of fatal crashes per million miles traveled, April 2001 to March 2002

9.3
16 years old

Number of Fatalities

Age

Taken from: Insurance Institute for Highway Safety/Highway Loss Data Institute/*Boston Globe*, June 2, 2006.

The push to revamp laws for young drivers gathered momentum . . . after numerous lawmakers said they were troubled by a spate of fatal accidents involving teenage drivers.

Last October [2005], teenage sisters Shauna and Meghan Murphy of Southborough were killed when their car hit a tree. In March [2006] two 16-year-olds from Reading, Amanda Nadeau and Scott Connolly, died on Route 128 in Wakefield, followed days later by a crash killing two Hopkinton siblings, Andrea, 17, and Joshua Goncalves, 10.

Teenagers Oppose Raising Driving Age

But teenagers became among the most vocal opponents of the effort saying that raising the driving age would be unfair and a hardship for those with jobs. Yesterday a majority of area high school students interviewed questioned the effort to make them wait a year longer for a license.

"There are a lot of immature knuckleheads out there, no matter what age they are," said J.J. Pena of Roxbury, 16, a student at Brook Farm Business and Service Career Academy in West Roxbury, who has a learner's permit. "You're still young when you're 17 1/2. I don't know that it will make things better."

Young drivers, along with elderly drivers, are the most likely to be involved in crashes. According to the Registry of Motor Vehicles, 30 percent of all 16-year-old drivers in Massachusetts get into serious accidents.

But some critics of the measure, including AAA [American Automobile Association] Southern New England, questioned whether increasing the minimum age would make a significant difference. They said the state would do more to increase safety by enhancing training of young drivers and enforcement of existing laws.

Many Contest Raising Driving Age

The wide range of opinion in the House became clear in recent days when Wagner was forced to consider 65 amendments to his bill, including a dozen that contested the proposal to raise the driving age.

"A lot of people were surprised by the number of amendments that came in," said state Representative Bradford R. Hill, an Ipswich Republican who introduced a broad amendment that would rewrite virtually all of Wagner's bill and keep the current driving age.

"There's nobody that wants to see this bill die, but we don't want to put out something that's an absolute joke," Hill said.

The bill, including raising the driving age, was narrowly approved by the Legislature's Joint Committee on Transportation. . . . But . . . swamped with hostile amendments, Wagner moved to delay debate on his proposal minutes before discussion was scheduled to begin. "With such a wide variance on the issue of age, the last thing we want to do is rush something through," he said.

In lieu of raising teen driving ages, many states have opted to increase the hours of on-road training in their state driver's education programs.

Hill, considered a leader in the House on driving-related issues, said he was skeptical of any age-change provision: "Seventeen-and-a-half was to me a deal-breaker. And I'm not convinced we need to move it up to 17."

Driving Safety Can Be Improved with Other Measures

Wagner said other provisions in his bill would improve driving safety by increasing the on-road training in driver's education classes from 6 hours to 15 hours, and by raising the parent-supervised driving requirement from 12 hours to 50.

"I think we'll try and achieve consensus around the provisions that deal with driving experience," said Wagner.

Wagner's proposal to raise the driving age . . . caused much discussion among the high school set. Lyuda Shriftman, 17, a junior at Needham High School said safe driving has little to do with age. "I think it's experience, not how old you are," she said. . . .

But Emily Britt, another 17-year-old junior at Needham High, acknowledged she talks on her cellphone and has some other unsafe driving habits. "If I'm in a hurry—I'm not going to lie—I do speed a little bit," she said.

Debora Louis, 17, of Dorchester, has decided not to seek a license yet, though she is old enough. Two years ago, she was asleep in the backseat of a car driven by her father when a loud boom jarred her awake. An oncoming car had hit them, injuring Louis's father. She was unhurt.

"Ever since that day, I promised myself I wouldn't drive until I got over that fear," said Louis, a student at Brook Farm Academy. "When we drive too close to cars, I get scared."

THREE

Graduated Driver Licensing Saves the Lives of Young Drivers

Insurance Institute for Highway Safety

In the following viewpoint the Insurance Institute for Highway Safety examines the main causes of fatal teen crashes and how a graduated licensing program can help reduce fatalities. Vehicle crashes are the leading cause of death among American teens, accounting for more than one-third of all deaths of sixteen- to eighteen-year-olds. Graduated licensing helps reduce crashes by imposing limits that grant new drivers privileges over an extended period of time. The limits are lifted gradually, so that young drivers have increased experience as they encounter more difficult driving situations, such as night driving and driving with a number of passengers in the vehicle.

Teen drivers have the highest crash risk of any age group. Per mile traveled, they have the highest involvement rates in crashes, from crashes involving property damage only to those that are fatal. The problem is worst among 16-year-olds, who have the most limited driving experience and an immaturity that often results in risk-taking behind the wheel. The characteristics of 16-year-olds' fatal crashes shed light on the problem:

Driver error: Compared with crashes of older drivers, those of 16-year-olds more often involve driver error.

Insurance Institute for Highway Safety, "Beginning Teenage Drivers," September 2006. Copyright © 1996–2006, Insurance Institute for Highway Safety, Highway Loss Data Institute. Reproduced by permission.

Speeding: 16-year-old drivers have a higher rate of crashes in which excessive speed is a factor.

Single-vehicle crashes: More of 16-year-olds' fatal crashes involve only the teen's vehicle. Typically these are high-speed crashes in which the driver lost control.

Passengers: 16-year-olds' fatal crashes are more likely to occur when other teenagers are in the car. The risk increases with every additional passenger.

Alcohol: Although this is a problem among drivers of all ages, it's actually less of a problem for 16-year-olds. Typically, less than

Teen drivers have the highest accident risk of any age group. Here, rescue workers give medical attention to two teens injured in a car crash.

15 percent of fatally injured 16-year-old drivers have blood alcohol concentrations of .08 grams per deciliter or greater. However, alcohol quickly becomes a problem in the later teen years.

Night driving: This is a high-risk activity for beginners. Per mile driven, the nighttime fatal crash rate for 16-year-olds is about twice as high as during the day.

Low belt use: Teenagers generally are less likely than adults to use safety belts.

Graduated Licenses Help Reduce Fatal Crashes

Teenagers perceive a driver's license as a ticket to freedom. It's momentous for parents, too. Though they are often aware of 16-year-olds' high crash risks, they're relieved not to have to chauffeur their children around anymore. But the price is steep. Crashes are the *leading cause of death* among American teens, accounting for more than one third of all deaths of 16- to 18-year-olds.

Percentage of Fatal Crashes by Characteristic, 2004

Driver Age	16	17–19	20–49
Driver error	78	69	55
Speeding	39	33	23
Single vehicle	52	45	39
3+ occupants	29	24	18
Drivers killed with .08+ BAC*	13	25	44

*Blood Alcohol Content

Taken from: Insurance Institute for Highway Safety, "Beginning Teenage Drivers," 2006.

An effective way to reduce this toll is to enact graduated licensing, under which driving privileges are phased in to restrict beginners' initial experience behind the wheel to lower-risk situations. The restrictions gradually are lifted, so teenagers are more experienced and mature when they get their full, unrestricted licenses.

Graduated systems that are well designed restrict night driving, limit teen passengers, set zero alcohol tolerance, and require a specified amount of supervised practice during the initial phase. Graduated licensing laws have reduced teens' crash rates in the United States, Canada, and New Zealand. But not all States have such laws, and the laws aren't all strong.

Rules Based on Graduated Licensing

With or without a graduated licensing law, parents can establish rules based on the graduated model. In particular:

Don't rely solely on driver education. High school driver education may be the most convenient way to learn skills, but it doesn't *necessarily* produce safer drivers. Poor skills aren't always to blame. Teen attitudes and decision-making matter more. Young people naturally tend to rebel. Teens often think they're immune to harm, so they don't use safety belts as much and they deliberately seek thrills like speeding. Training and education don't change these tendencies. Peer influence is great but parents have much more influence than they are typically given credit for.

Know the law. Become familiar with restrictions on beginning drivers. Enforce the rules. . . .

Restrict night driving. Most young drivers' nighttime fatal crashes occur from 9 p.m. to midnight, so teens shouldn't drive much later than 9. The problem isn't just that such driving requires more skill. Late outings tend to be recreational, and even teens who usually follow the rules can be easily distracted or encouraged to take risks.

Restrict passengers. Teen passengers in a vehicle can distract a beginning driver and/or lead to greater risk-taking. Because young drivers often transport their friends, there's a teen passenger problem as well as a teen driver problem. About 6 of every 10 teenage passenger deaths (59%) during 2003 occurred in crashes with a teen driver. While night driving with passengers is particularly lethal, many fatal crashes with teen passengers occur during the day. The best policy is to restrict teenage passengers, especially multiple teens, all the time.

Supervise practice driving. Take an active role in helping your teenager learn how to drive. Plan a series of practice sessions in a wide variety of situations, including night driving. Give beginners time to work up to challenges like driving in heavy traffic or on the freeway. Supervised practice should be spread over at least six months and continue even after a teenager graduates from a learner's permit to a restricted or full license.

Remember that you're a role model. New drivers learn a lot by example, so practice safe driving. Teens with crashes and violations often have parents with poor driving records.

Require safely belt use. Don't assume that belt use when you're in the car with your 16-year-old means belts will be used all the time, especially when your child is out with peers. Remember that belt use is lower among teenagers than older people. Insist on belts all the time.

Prohibit drinking. Make it clear that it's illegal and highly dangerous for a teenager to drink alcohol. While alcohol isn't a factor in most crashes of 16-year-old drivers, even small amounts of alcohol are impairing for teens.

Choose vehicles for safety, not image. Teenagers should drive vehicles that reduce their chances of a crash and offer protection in case they do crash. For example, small cars don't offer the best protection in a crash. Avoid cars with performance images that might encourage speeding. Avoid trucks and sport utility vehicles—the smaller ones, especially, are more prone to roll over.

FOUR

Laws Restricting Teen Drivers Are Key to Reducing Crash Risk

Jacqueline S. Gillan

In the following viewpoint Jacqueline S. Gillan maintains that legislative advocacy is critical to reducing teen driving deaths. She draws from the research of numerous sources to present an argument for state and federal governments to encourage comprehensive four-element graduated driver license (GDL) laws for all states. As of March 2006, only the state of Nevada had all four elements in place; in Gillan's view, many states had incomplete or nonexistent GDL life-saving laws. Gillan has over thirty years' experience in the fields of transportation planning and government relations. She is vice president of Advocates for Highway and Auto Safety, a coalition of consumer, health, safety, medical, and insurance companies and organizations promoting laws to reduce highway deaths.

Motor vehicle crashes are the leading cause of death for 15–20-year-olds. In 2004, 7,898 15–20-year-old drivers were involved in fatal crashes, 3,620 drivers in this age group were killed and an additional 303,000 were injured. By any measure, this represents a public health epidemic.

Data show that teenage drivers are overrepresented in motor vehicle crashes, far exceeding their percentage among licensed

Jacqueline S. Gillan, "Legislative Advocacy Is Key to Addressing Teen Driving Deaths," *Injury Prevention*, vol. 12, 2006, pp. 144–148. Copyright © 2006 BMJ Publishing Group Ltd. Reproduced by permission.

drivers. Even though teenage drivers as a group drive fewer miles per year than drivers in other age groups, teenage drivers are involved in fatal crashes at more than double the rate of the rest of the population (per 100,000 licensed drivers), and their involvement rate in all crashes is more than three times that of the general population of licensed drivers.

Teens Are Involved in More Accidents for Various Reasons

A number of factors contribute to this situation. While younger drivers in general tend to have good eyesight, reflexes, and hand-eye coordination, they frequently lack the experience and good judgment necessary in critical driving situations. Teenage

Chairs representing seventy-one teens killed in Tennessee traffic accidents are shown behind officials announcing changes to the state's graduated licensing program. Many states are enacting graduated licensing programs.

drivers are less likely than adults to accurately perceive danger and more likely to commit driving errors that lead to a crash, such as driving at excessive speeds in the prevailing conditions or overcompensating during sudden maneuvers. In addition, they have a greater propensity to engage in risk-taking behaviors, such as speeding and driving recklessly, compared to other age groups.

Teenage drivers are more likely to be involved in single-vehicle crashes and crashes with peers, especially male peers. Drivers under the age of 20 are also overrepresented in rollover fatalities. Finally, teenagers are statistically less likely to be wearing seat belts either as drivers or passengers of motor vehicles. These factors all contribute to teenage drivers having the highest crash and fatality rate of all age groups of drivers, a finding that applies even when the data for male and female teenage drivers are disaggregated [separated].

Graduated Driver Licensing Laws Reduce Teen Deaths and Injuries

It has been repeatedly documented that young drivers are at increased risk when there are one or more teen passengers on board and vehicle operation occurs during the higher crash risk hours of darkness, especially on weekends. Every state and foreign country that has instituted some version of GDL (Graduated Driver Licensing) has experienced success in reducing the frequency of teen driver collisions that occur when teenage drivers are provided unrestricted, full licensure especially when 16 or 17 years of age. In fact, as Thomas Dee and his co-authors pointed out in 2005, no research findings on the effects of GDL in any state or foreign country that has adopted some version of the licensing control on teen driving has failed to find positive effects.

Both federal and state legislative actions requiring GDL, coupled with public education on the benefits of GDL, are necessary to lower teenage driver and teenage occupant crash deaths and injuries. For years, government-sponsored slogans and industry public relations campaigns focused on the dangers of drinking and driving did not achieve sustained or consistent declines in the number of annual drunk driving fatalities. When safety groups, particularly Mothers Against Drunk Driving (MADD), changed the focus to enactment of state and federal laws such as the minimum 21-year-old drinking age, tougher penalties for impaired driving, reducing the blood alcohol concentration level to 0.08% in every state, combined with education and enforcement of these laws, drunk driving deaths and injuries began to steadily drop. From 2003 to 2004, national alcohol-related motor vehicle crash deaths fell from 12,997 to 12,636, a 2.8% reduction in a single year. Likewise, alcohol-related motor vehicle fatalities fell by 2.9% from 2002 to 2003.

Four Key Elements of GDL Laws Are Required

Similarly, Advocates [for Highway and Auto Safety] is working to bring about uniformity in state GDL laws with this two-pronged strategy to accelerate state adoption of laws that have the following four elements:

1. *Minimum six-month holding period*. During this period an adult licensed driver must supervise a new driver at all times. In a graduated system, an extended learner's period is essential to provide the opportunity for extensive supervised on-road practice in a variety of conditions. The developing consensus is that a minimum of six months is reasonable and necessary.

2. *Thirty to 50 hours of supervised driving*. A new driver should complete 30–50 hours of behind-the-wheel training with an adult licensed driver. This again aims to ensure a minimum amount of supervised on-road practice in a variety of conditions.

3. *Night-time driving restriction*. Under Advocates' optimal GDL program, unsupervised driving should be prohibited from 10pm to 5am. Night-time driving is especially risky for young beginners and young people in general.

4. *Passenger restriction*. The number of teenage passengers that should be allowed to accompany a teen driver without adult supervision is one non-familial teenager. This also is a recom-

mendation of the National Transportation Safety Board, while others recommend more stringent restrictions.

As of March 2006, only the state of Nevada has all four elements of an optimal graduated license law, and 18 states and the District of Columbia have three of the four optimal provisions. There is a patchwork quilt of teenage driving laws across the country, and too many states have too few of these life-saving laws. This means that many states have incomplete GDL programs that cannot achieve the benefits of a careful, three-step system of driver licensing.

Advocates for Highway and Auto Safety Makes Recommendations

Each year, Advocates identifies several states that have no components of a comprehensive GDL law or weak laws that need to be upgraded and improved. Working with state and local coalitions, victim advocacy groups, and elected officials, Advocates assists in efforts to promote passage of GDL laws. For example, Advocates' staff works to identify sponsors of GDL legislation, seeks the support of governors, other elected officials and public opinion leaders, attracts media attention by encouraging press events and editorials, and reaches out to victims/survivors of teen driving crashes and helps them to focus their interest and energy in the legislative debate.

Furthermore, in order to push efforts in state legislatures to enact GDL laws, Advocates issues a report in late December or early January before the beginning of most state legislative sessions assessing state progress in adopting about 14 critical highway safety laws in the areas of adult occupant protection, child passenger safety, teen driving, and impaired driving. These are laws which Advocates views as necessary to effectively reduce motor vehicle deaths and injuries. The report, *Roadmap to Highway Safety Laws*, evaluates states relative to neighboring states and the rest of the nation in passage of these laws. The evaluation of GDL laws has helped the public, the media, and elected officials identify those states lacking some of the most fundamental laws protecting teens, which in turn has been a catalyst for strengthening GDL laws. Another strategy used by Advocates to encourage states to enact a comprehensive GDL law is the passage of federal legislation. Some of the most important highway safety laws affecting teen driving and uniformly adopted by every state resulted from the United States Congress legislating in order to spur state enactment. These include the national minimum 21-year-old drinking age, the zero tolerance blood alcohol concentration (BAC) law for underage drinking and driving, and the 0.08% BAC law. Uniform state adoption of these three laws resulted from the passage of federal legislation directing states to adopt these lifesaving laws within a specified time period or be penalized millions of dollars in federal highway construction funding.

Youth Driver Training Programs Do Not Replace GDL Laws

Despite the proven track record of GDL, there is still significant opposition to the lifesaving benefits of this rational approach to reducing young driver crash risk, including state legislatures resisting enactment of the GDL concept or of strengthening current programs. These improvements comprise, for example, more restrictions on teen passengers. In some cases, GDL opponents still claim that driver education and training programs can produce the same crash reduction fatality benefits as GDL; however, this view has no real support. Youth driver training courses can teach basic vehicle control skills, but extensive research has shown repeatedly that high school driver education, for example, does not lead to lower crash involvement rates. This is because many other variables affect young drivers behind the wheel that result in increased crash rates.

Despite driver education, a study conducted for the Commonwealth of Virginia, for example, showed that for use of alcohol and other drugs, speeding, reckless driving, improper driving, high risk behavior, seat belt violations, and administrative violations, the percentage of convicted drivers in their late teens was several times higher than for any other age group. No study conducted in more than 30 years has shown that teenage

"Careless Driver," cartoon by Dan Reynolds. CartoonStock.com.

driver education effectively reduces either the rate or the severity of young driver crash involvement.

Research Shows Intensive Driver Training Is Not Effective

In fact, many authors and researchers point out that young driver education usually enables teenage drivers to gain unrestricted licensure at earlier ages when their risk of violations or crashes is much higher than older drivers, while also encouraging them to increase their exposure to crash involvement by driving more miles, longer hours, and more often at night at a younger age. Even more disturbing are the results of several well-known evaluation studies that have shown that intensive driver training courses for novice drivers result in graduates who actually have higher collision rates than those without such training, especially when the subjects are young drivers. This research, along with recent work in the area of human brain development, has provided the basis for calls to increase the age of licensure.

Other studies in the US, Canada, Scandinavia, Australia, and New Zealand have also shown that driver education courses produce no long-term beneficial advantages in reducing either the frequency or the severity of crash involvements. The record of research findings is therefore clear that driver education of young teen drivers does not decrease crash rates.

In contrast, GDL systems, especially the programs that contain the most desirable features of a three-step progression in driving privileges, curtailment of night-time driving, and prohibitions on carrying other teens as passengers, are repeatedly proven as lifesaving public policy actions by reducing the high crash exposure of younger teen drivers during the time when they are least able to rely on mature judgment and experience to drive safely.

Part of Advocates' approach to promoting GDL legislation has been to address the education needs of both state and federal legislators regarding the research on both GDL and driver education courses. This has greatly complicated the task because many state and federal officials (as well as parents) believe that driver education courses alone are effective, and because driver education in many school districts is a well-established part of secondary school education.

Public Opinion Polls Indicate Support for GDL Laws

One of the most successful strategies used by Advocates to counter opposition to federal and state GDL and other highway safety laws are public opinion polls. Advocates has commissioned independent pollster Lou Harris to conduct several public opinion polls over the past 10 years to assess public attitudes on a variety of issues related to highway, auto, and truck safety including teen driving.

In a public opinion poll conducted by Lou Harris for Advocates in 2001, several questions concerning some of the most controversial features of GDL laws were asked. Harris polled a cross section of 1,001 US adults (18 years and older) on a wide range of safety issues including questions on teen driver restrictions. By large majorities, the public wants enforced restrictions placed on young drivers before and initially after they receive their licenses. The poll indicated that there is broad support for teenage drivers to complete at least 30–50 hours of practice driving accompanied by an adult (95% support), requiring a six-month learner's permit (92% support), and limiting night-time driving as well as teen passengers (74% support). However, when the public was surveyed about increasing the driving age above the current minimum age, a 54–42% margin opposed the suggestion. At present, the minimum driving age allowed in the US varies widely between states and is considerably younger than in most industrialized nations.

FIVE

Driver Education Needs Standards and Support

Eddie Wren

In the following viewpoint Eddie Wren summarizes the 2003 Public Forum on Driver Education and Training conducted by the National Transportation Safety Board. He addresses the effectiveness of driver education as stated by speakers from numerous organizations involved with transportation, public and driver education, transportation research, and safety councils. Two of the speakers are high school students discussing their experiences in school driver's education programs. Wren points out that more young people are killed on American highways than in Iraq, and that the United States made poor progress compared with many other countries in reducing the death toll on highways between 1992 and 2001. Wren is the executive director of Drive and Stay Alive, Inc., and director of policy for Advanced Drivers of America.

Many reports show no evidence that Driver Education actually benefits young drivers in terms of any reduction in crashes or casualties. And Driver Education is not an effective substitute for supervised, practical driving experience.

These were just two of the points made by the first speaker at the NTSB [National Transportation Safety Board] Public Forum on Driver Education and Training—Dr. Jim Nichols—who also quoted the late Professor Pat Waller of the University of Michigan Transportation Research Institute, who said: "It is ridiculous to assume that thirty hours Driver Education is going to affect driver safety."

But the argument wasn't one-sided. Some later speakers at the Washington DC conference rallied around the educationalist flag.

The catalyst which brought about this event was a tragic accident ten months ago—January 2003—in Montana, in which three young students and their 49-year-old Driver Education teacher all died when their car got into the path of an oncoming tractor/semi trailer (a.k.a. an "articulated wagon" in other countries). The car driver was just 14 years old.

Driver Education Effectiveness Has Been Overstated

"In Driver Education we have made many big mistakes and the biggest was to overstate our effectiveness," said Dr. Allen Robinson, Director of the Highway Safety Center at the Indiana University of Pennsylvania. "Early claims were fifty percent then ten percent reductions in teen fatalities but clearly both of these claims were ridiculous. No one factor can cause such reductions."

The greatest benefit of Graduated Driver Licensing, he added, is that it has a combination of factors which work together to enhance the safety of young drivers.

Sean McLaurin, of the National Highway Traffic Safety Administration (NHTSA), was swiftly able to sober the mood of the forum by repeating one statistic that most of the delegates would already have known: From 1999 through 2002, almost exactly 26,000 teenagers were killed on America's roads.

More Young People Are Killed on Highways than in Iraq

"It is a tragedy," said David Huff, of Montana Driver Education, later, "that we are losing young soldiers in Iraq. But it is an even greater tragedy that we turn a blind eye to the [much larger] number of young people that are killed every day on our highways.

"If you ask teens why they are doing Driver Education, more than ninety percent of them will say: 'So that I can get a driver's license.' Most of the rest will say: 'So that I don't crash Dad's car.' Almost none of them even consider safety. Two studies into Driver Education by the NHTSA were disappointing," he continued, "and they led to the eventual end of the Agency's use of '402' funds [highway safety funds distributed by the federal government] to support the Driver Education program."

But at this point Mr. McLaurin raised what is undoubtedly the greatest paradox and indeed the greatest frustration of the whole issue: "Some school sports programs cost parents $900 and they willingly pay, but many parents complain to me that they had to pay $300 towards driving lessons!" It would appear that many parents don't recognize the futility of sporting skills—or music, or drama, or even academic prowess itself—if, for want of better training, their child is killed in a road accident. And, tragically, this happens several thousand times a year.

Ways Must Be Found to Improve Driver Training

Driver Education is not going away, McLaurin assured the delegates, but ways to improve it must be found. "Would you let someone re-plumb your house if they only had thirty hours' classroom and six hours' practical training as a plumber? It is only after a kid has learned that the brake pedal is on the left, and the gas pedal is on the right, and how to stay off the sidewalk that they can start to absorb driving advice in any greater depth."

In the subsequent "question and answer" session, Mr. McLaurin was asked about standardizing driving tests in the USA, especially as some places give tests where the new driver does not even have to drive on a public road and merely has to drive around a parking lot. "There are as many systems as there are states, and even counties," he responded. "It *is* needed, but in the current political climate it is not going to happen. We definitely need it."

In many states new drivers learn driving skills without ever leaving a parking lot. Attempts are being made to standardize driver training throughout the country.

International comparisons for driver training and testing were in order. Dr. Stefan Siegrist, from the Swiss Council for Accident Prevention, told us all that there is evidence of benefits from increased training under controlled circumstances and from the introduction of what he called "second phase training."

"Two-phase training," he told us, "is used in six European countries and it is giving particularly good results in Finland." After classroom and behind-the-wheel training, students take a written test and a driving test, after which they receive a provisional driver's license. But only after further compulsory, theoretical and practical training can they apply for a full driver's license.

When asked, Dr. Siegrist told the delegates that driving tests in Europe are much more comprehensive and difficult than those in the USA, but he added that this in itself was not the cause of the improved safety results, rather it was the fact that the harder tests force instructors to do a much better job. . . .

The Brussels-based "Organisation for Economic Co-operation and Development" (OECD), administers the "International Road Traffic and Accident Database" (IRTAD) for this very reason. The Database shows relevant statistics from 28 OECD member countries, and the USA is in a very poor 23rd place with a death rate of 15.2 per one-hundred-thousand people, by comparison with the best countries' rates of around 6 per hundred-thousand. . . .

Driving Programs Should Be Regulated

State Programs were [also discussed during the forum], and Elizabeth Weaver-Shepard was first up, on behalf of the Idaho Department of Education.

"Idaho would like to see national standards for Driver Education," she said, early in her presentation. "Driver Education lessons have been pushed out of the school day and so they start as soon as 6am and run as late as 9pm," she added later.

Commercial driving schools [that provide Driver Education] follow no state requirements in terms of curriculum and standards. I believe [this should be regulated]."

Mrs. Weaver-Shepard presented a good case for Driver Education but one point on which some delegates—the writer included—disagreed with her was her stated belief that reductions in crashes or fatalities are not a valid criterion by which to judge the success or otherwise of Driver Ed.

David Huff made an early comment that "Successful Driver Education must address not only the needs of teenagers but also the lifelong teaching of parents—the role models."

"Driver Education in the United States is deplorable!" he added, with obvious feeling. "To overcome existing shortfalls, there must exist:

- A clear definition of a model driver
- A learner-centered curriculum
- Standards and programs for teacher preparation
- An aligned licensing process
- Program standards for *all* programs
- State oversight and management
- Accountability, corrective measures, and consequences
- Lifelong learning
- Other education messages
- Federal policy and fiscal support

"Much Driver Education [in the USA] today is based on archaic systems," he said. . . .

Student Ideas on Improving Driver Ed

At this point in the forum, it could be said that two well-meaning and thoroughly honest students who spoke shot the proponents of Driver Education in the foot. Kayla Craddick, from Lubbock, Texas, came first, but in among all her good comments about Driver Ed. she stated that she "learned more about [her] instructor and his funny stories than [she] did about driving." And that she "had to learn basic things later that [she] should have been taught." And "Some areas were covered too quickly. It was assumed that [she] already knew things."

She delivered the coup de grâce [final blow] when she said "I didn't even have to do all my required driving time."

Miss Craddick, however, then turned her situation to advantage and gave a very thought-provoking list of things that could be done to improve Driver Education from the point of view of a student driver:

- More driving time should be required with parents or instructor
- The D.E. teacher should let parents know what aspects their child is having difficulty with so that it may be practiced

- Instruction should touch on related subjects such as road rage, the dangers of over-correcting, bad weather driving, aspects of defensive driving, etc.
- Students should be tested on actual situations
- Higher scores should be required for a test pass (She had commented earlier that the test was too easy.)
- The age at which a license could be obtained should be raised
- It should be made clear to students that driving is a privilege that can easily be taken away
- Instructors should be made more accountable
- Students should be shown more videos and told more real-life stories (She added that "kids are more likely to listen to their peers than to adults so kids' own stories should be on videos.")
- Police officers should be asked to attend Driver Ed. classes to talk about driving laws, etc.

Driver Ed Should Be More than a Fun Class

"When I was sixteen I went into Driver Education to get my license. That was all I was there for," [said student Brad Wells]. "I had fun—it was a fun class. It won't put you to sleep like math and English!"

He told the delegates that he didn't like the way the material was presented and that the text book seemed out of date; it seemed "eighties." And he added that the things presented "seemed so easy for something so important."

Mr. Wells was later asked how much time he had spent driving the car, with his instructor. He replied "After twenty hours in class, I did four hours [driving] with the instructor but it was just driving around. I learned much more from my parents than I did from the instructor. I learned how to drive on freeways from my Dad. We drive into Salt Lake City a lot."

He, too, commented on what he felt was needed:
- More use of modern technology
- More parental involvement (and parents must be made aware of their responsibility as role models)

- Tighter enforcement of laws, otherwise kids hear lots of empty threats—they learn that there's no disciplining

He also commented on driving itself, from a teenage boy's point of view:

- Things aren't the same when Mom and Dad aren't watching (the stated implication being that rules swiftly go out of the window)
- A young driver's behavior changes depending on the type of passenger they have in the car
- Many teens think they are immortal—"It's never gonna happen to them; they [think they] are good drivers!"
- Many parents don't realize the impact they have as model drivers (over the kid's lifetime, not just the last few months before the test)
- Some teens don't think that driving laws apply to them. They think they can get out of anything.

Tellingly Mr. Wells finished his presentation with the comment: "As one of the things I've done, in the National Student Safety Program [NSSP], we did a mock car crash. We even had a helicopter out there. But a lot of kids just laughed it off. They still spun donuts on the parking lot—they still sped down bus lanes."

The eternal challenge faced by road safety educators around the world had come to the fore once again. As hard as the upper echelons of ADTSEA [American Driver & Traffic Safety Education Association] are undoubtedly working to improve the effectiveness and image of Driver Education in the USA, it must have been aggravating for them to hear the shortcomings outlined by these two young people. . . .

Driver Training Courses Should Be Standardized

Mr. Keith Russell, the executive director of the [DSAA] Driving School Association of the America's [also addressed] the delegates. He stated that there are problems with Driver Education in the public school and private school systems. Twenty-three states, he told us, have no Driver Education at all, and in some of those states that do, the standard is poor. He also addressed the point that road test standards vary greatly from one state to another.

The DSAA want a national mandate for Driver Education. They also wish to see two-segment driver education—the first part to focus on maneuvers and compliance, and the second part on cognitive skills, risk recognition and behavioral modification. A national standard for road testing and a national mandate for safer vehicles are also on the list of DSAA goals.

"It is important people understand that Driver Education is only a starting point from which to begin a lifetime of learning to drive. This naturally ensures our independence and all of the freedoms we hold dear," said Mr. Russell.

"We [also] need public service announcements, just like we used to have when we were kids. We need them around the clock. We need to let people know how many are being killed and injured [in road crashes]," he added.

Mr. Wayne Tully, CEO of the National Driver Training Institute, said: "Driver Education and a test pass give parents and teens a false sense of security. . . . The biggest mistake in the Driver Education industry is the concept that you can teach a young person to drive safely with just six hours behind the wheel. . . . Student drivers should have at least fifty hours behind the wheel."

The drift of Tully's general remarks were echoed by the next speaker, Frederick Mottola, executive director of the National Institute of Driver Behavior, who said that most drivers have all the manipulative skills necessary to drive a vehicle but that what they don't have are the cognitive abilities.

It's Time to Re-focus on Driver Education

Troy Costales is the Transportation Safety Division Manager for Oregon, and the Governors' Highway Safety Association representative for the state. He got to the crux of the matter when he said: "I suggest to you that Graduated Driver Licensing is the last breath of life for Driver Education. If we don't take advantage of it we may lose it forever. . . . The Governors' Highway Safety Association firmly believes that the time is right to re-focus on Driver Education.

"Somebody, somewhere, has to be charged with the responsibility, at a national level. . . . We must change the culture of what it is to be a teen driver in this nation. It is *not* a right. . . . It needs to be earned."

Mr. Charles Butler, who has been with the American Automobile Association [AAA] since 1976, gave a detailed summary of AAA policy. It included many pertinent points but the two most in line with the direction of this summary were:

- To increase instructional focus on safer driving practices, and
- To implement uniform instructor qualification standards

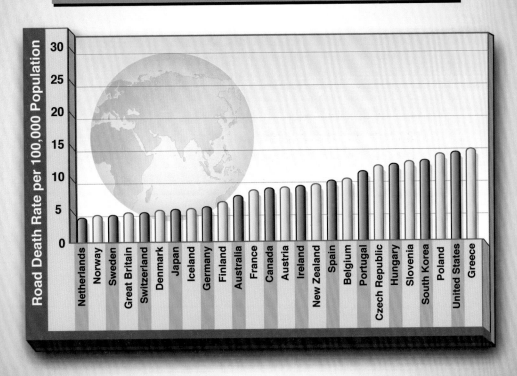

International Road Safety Comparisons, 2005

Road Death Rate per 100,000 Population

Netherlands, Norway, Sweden, Great Britain, Switzerland, Denmark, Japan, Iceland, Germany, Finland, Australia, France, Canada, Austria, Ireland, New Zealand, Spain, Belgium, Portugal, Czech Republic, Hungary, Slovenia, South Korea, Poland, United States, Greece

Taken from: "International Road Safety Comparisons: The 2005 Report," Australian Transport Safety Bureau, May 2007.

He also outlined some AAA research, giving the principle causes for young driver crashes:

- 44% involve visual errors
- 23% involve attention
- 21% involve excess speed
- 10% involve poor judgment of space
- 9% involve emergency situations
- 8% involve [a lack of] basic control …

The United States Has a Comparatively Poor Safety Record

[The United States] lies in 24th position out of 30 countries for the *per capita* death rate, and in 10th position out of 24 countries for the Vehicle Miles Traveled (VMT) death rate (2002 data), but in addition, a study of the historical data shows that America's position in these results has remained relatively unchanged since at least 1988. Indeed, of the 24 countries for which advances can be measured over the period 1992–2001, the USA made the least progress of any, having a reduction in the overall per capita death toll of just 4 percent, compared to reductions of up to 39 percent in the [other countries]. . . .

We are making these comments not to cause offence but to make the point that as long as the seemingly common yet entirely erroneous belief exists that America has the safest roads, the more likely it is that complacency will have an adverse effect on public perception and political actions.

SIX

Preventing Drugged Driving Saves Teen Lives

Melanie Marciano

> In the following viewpoint the author explains that mixed
> messages about the safety of marijuana can lead to teen
> drugged driving, which in turn can lead to motor-vehicle
> crashes and fatalities. The author addresses marijuana's
> adverse effect on driving and how parents and young people
> can help prevent these motor-vehicle accidents, which are
> the leading cause of death for teens. She asserts that parents
> must educate themselves as well as talk with their teens
> and monitor their activities. Melanie Marciano has worked
> as a correspondent for United Press International.

Mixed messages about the safety of marijuana are leading to
teen drugged driving and parents need to intervene and
communicate the dangers of that practice, drug and safety experts
said [on December 2, 2004].

The month of December was declared by President George W.
Bush to be National Drunk and Drugged Driving Prevention
Month. The White House Office of National Drug Control Policy
[ONDCP] put together a news conference to make clear the need for
teen education on the danger of driving under the influence of drugs.

"There is a great deal of ignorance about drug impaired driving," said ONDCP Director John Walters. Teens have been

reported to believe it is safer to drive while under the influence of marijuana than alcohol, panel members said. The belief is contributed to by misperceptions of the drug's damaging properties, Walters explained.

Drugged Driving Contributes to Young Driver Deaths

The National Highway Traffic Safety Administration details marijuana's adverse affect on driving: decreased car-handling performance, increased reaction times, impaired time and dis-

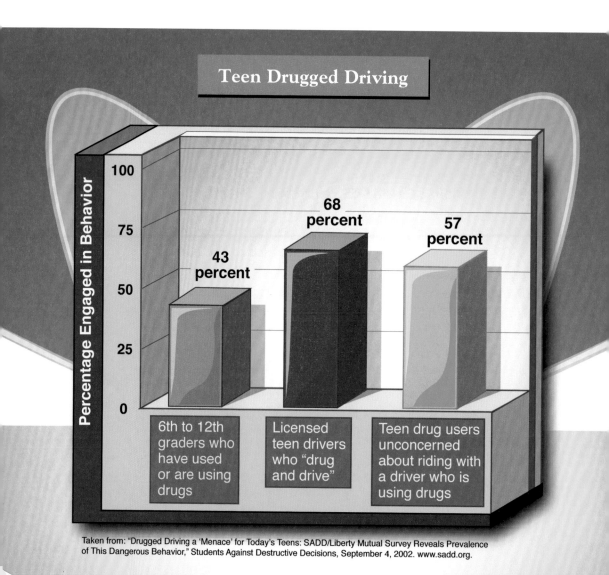

Teen Drugged Driving

Percentage Engaged in Behavior

- 43 percent: 6th to 12th graders who have used or are using drugs
- 68 percent: Licensed teen drivers who "drug and drive"
- 57 percent: Teen drug users unconcerned about riding with a driver who is using drugs

Taken from: "Drugged Driving a 'Menace' for Today's Teens: SADD/Liberty Mutual Survey Reveals Prevalence of This Dangerous Behavior," Students Against Destructive Decisions, September 4, 2002. www.sadd.org.

tance estimation, inability to maintain headway, lateral travel, subjective sleepiness, declining motor skills and impaired sustained attention have all been reported. Combining alcohol and marijuana intensify the effects.

"Motor-vehicle crashes is the leading cause of death in teens," said Dr. Jeffrey Runge, administrator of the National Highway Traffic Safety Administration. When lack of experience is combined with drugs and alcohol the result can be fatal, he added. Combating the problem of teens driving under the influence starts in the home, Runge said.

Parents need to fight the notion that it's too late or nothing can be done during the years that youth struggle for independence. "Far too often parents fall victim to the myth of inevitability," said Stephen Wallace, chairman of Students Against Drunk Driving [now Students Against Destructive Decisions]. By educating themselves, talking with teens, monitoring the activities of their children, encouraging positive activities such as sports or volunteering and not giving up, parents can play a huge role in keeping kids from drugs, Wallace said.

Mixed Messages About the Safety of Marijuana Contribute to the Problem

Parents and adults are often guilty of generating such mixed messages by facilitating, encouraging, but mostly ignoring, teen marijuana use, Wallace said. "Adults and parents need to take a hard look in the mirror and realize what messages they are sending to children," Wallace advised.

Adding to the confusion among teens on the safety of marijuana use is the availability of information that advocates the drug. A simple Internet search will turn up sites that refute the negative consequences of marijuana on driving, such as The Family Council on Drug Awareness.

The Family Council's Web site published this message: "Driving under the influence of any drug is generally discouraged, but studies have always indicated that marijuana has only a negligible effect on drivers who are experienced with its effects. The reason seems to be that, while there is a minor reduction in reaction

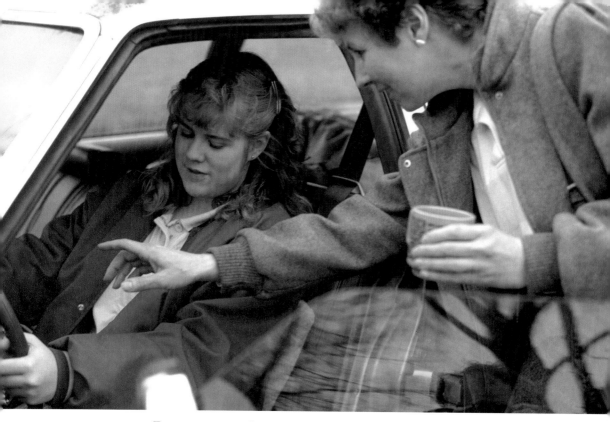

Parents must take an active role in their teens' driving education to counteract the effects of peer pressure from their friends and fellow students.

times similar to being a few years older than the driver's current age, there is a sense of 'paranoia' that leads to slower and more cautious driving."

The lack of studies of the prevalence of marijuana-related accidents also adds to the misperception of the danger of its use. Panelists said they regretted that they only have individual studies of accidents. Runge emphasized the country's need to look at prevalence. Panelists said they hoped that testing for specifically driving under the influence of marijuana would increase.

Drugged Driving Accidents Are Preventable

More drug and alcohol-influenced accidents occur during the holidays. Walters encouraged parents, the most important influence on teen's perception of drug use, to talk [during the] holiday season to teens.

In a statement released [December 2, 2004], Bush renewed his support of safe driving and behavior. "Individuals across our country can help prevent drunk and drugged driving by encouraging responsible actions, identifying sober designated drivers and educating young people about safe, substance-free driving behavior. Working together, all Americans can make our roads safer and save lives by preventing drunk and drugged driving," Bush said.

SEVEN

Cell Phones Are a Dangerous Distraction to Teen Drivers

Tom Chorneau and Michael Cabanatuan

Tom Chorneau and Michael Cabanatuan, *San Francisco Chronicle* staff writers, prepared the following viewpoint following the September 2007 passage of California's law prohibiting sixteen- and seventeen-year-olds from using cell phones, PDAs, and pagers while driving. Lawmakers acknowledge that cell phones are a major source of distraction for all drivers, but teens were particularly cited by the bill because, as Governor Arnold Schwarzenegger explains in the viewpoint, they are more easily distracted and have a slower reaction time due to their inexperience as drivers. California was not the first state to enact laws around mobile communication devices, according to the authors: fifteen other states, as well as Washington, D.C., already had them in place.

Allan Quach says he talks on his cell phone while driving, but tries to chat only with parents or friends who urgently need to talk to him. But minors like him won't be able to do that much longer, at least not legally.

California Enacts Law for Cell Phone Use While Driving

Come July 1, [2008], thousands of 16- and 17-year-olds in California will be prohibited from using cell phones, PDAs, laptops and pagers while driving, under a bill signed [September 13, 2007], by Gov. Arnold Schwarzenegger.

"It's going to make it harder to pick somebody up or take important phone calls—like an interview (for a job) or if something happened in your family," Quach, a student at Galileo High, said Thursday on his cell phone as he drove his car. Quach, 17, will turn 18 days before the law kicks in, so the restriction won't apply to him.

Many states have passed laws against the use of cell phones while driving because they are a major distraction among drivers, especially teens.

But Schwarzenegger and other backers of the law say there is increasing evidence that cell phones and other "mobile service devices" are a major source of distraction among all drivers, but especially teens, who are also the motorists most likely to have accidents.

Teens cited under SB33, authored by state Sen. Joe Simitian, D-Palo Alto, face a fine of $20 for a first offense and $50 each time after that. Officials said traffic officers will not be allowed to pull drivers over simply because of a cell phone infraction, and violations will not count as part of the traffic safety point system. Emergency calls will be exempt.

Fifteen other states and the District of Columbia have similar restrictions on teenage drivers.

Some Teens Use Cell Phones Inappropriately When Driving

Bay Area teenagers interviewed Thursday said they aren't sure the new regulations are fair.

"That's insane—it's madness," said Cameron Young of San Francisco, who, at 13, has a few years before he can get his license. "No technology? I'm speechless. Not cool, not cool at all."

Berkeley High School senior Will Kruse, who will turn 18 before the law kicks in, hadn't heard of the measure until Thursday and wasn't happy about it.

"Cell phones are such a big part of our society now," he said, although he acknowledged that he's seen some of his peers doing "crazy stuff" while driving. "I know a lot of my friends text message when they drive," he said. "You have to look down a lot while you're driving to do that."

Schwarzenegger, whose eldest daughter turned 16 [in 2006] and began driving, said teens need special protection. "The simple fact is that teenage drivers are more easily distracted," he said [September 13, 2007] at a bill-signing ceremony at Sequoia High School in Redwood City. "They are young, inexperienced and have a slower reaction time."

In a recent survey by AAA [American Automobile Association] and *Seventeen* magazine, about a third of the teenagers polled admitted to being distracted when driving while either sending text messages or talking on cell phones. A National Highway Traffic Safety Administration study found that 8 percent of drivers ages 16 to 24 used a handheld phone during daylight hours in 2004, compared with 5 percent in 2002 and 3 percent in 2000.

The governor's office reported that highway crashes are the leading cause of death among 16- to 20-year-olds, while highway accidents are the cause of 44 percent of teen deaths in the United States each year.

Cars and Cell Phones Can Be a Deadly Mix

Simitian, who wrote a law passed [in 2006] that requires the use of hands-free devices for drivers of all ages beginning July 1 [2008], said he believes that cell phones pose the greatest risk to drivers—especially teens. Under the law signed Thursday, teenage drivers will not be able to use even hands-free devices while driving.

"I understand that access to a set of car keys and a cell phone are a rite of passage for teenagers, but the combination can prove deadly," he said. "The message we need to be sending now is that the two don't mix."

Some Experts Disagree

But some transportation experts said there's still no strong data linking cell phones with crashes.

Matt Sundeen, transportation analyst with the National Council of State Legislatures, said crash sites usually include physical evidence of a cause such as drunken driving or speeding. He said accidents involving cell phone use are usually self-reported by the victim or by witnesses and thus might not be accurate or complete.

Some Students Actively Support Cell Phone Restrictions

While many teenagers oppose the new law, a group of eighth-graders in Granite Bay (Placer County) actively supported it.

Students in Craig Cook's history class analyzed Simitian's bill this year and argued over its merits. They overwhelmingly supported the

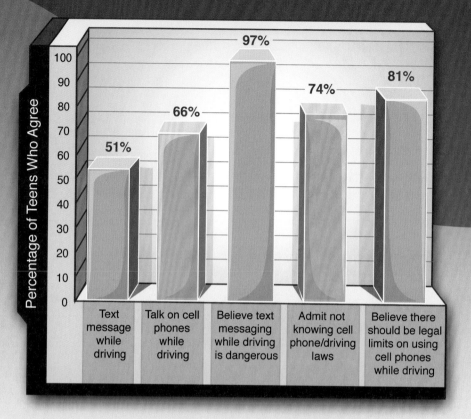

Teen Views on Cell Phone Use While Driving

Percentage of Teens Who Agree

- Text message while driving — 51%
- Talk on cell phones while driving — 66%
- Believe text messaging while driving is dangerous — 97%
- Admit not knowing cell phone/driving laws — 74%
- Believe there should be legal limits on using cell phones while driving — 81%

Taken from: Rocky Mountain Insurance Information Association, "Survey Shows Colorado Teens Text While Driving," November 13, 2007. www.rmiia.org.

bill and submitted their arguments to the Legislature during hearings in May [2007].

"It surprised me," said Cook. "I try as a teacher not to assume too much, and you'd expect most of the kids would think of this as a horrible intrusion in their lives. But by a 2-to-1 vote, they supported the bill."

Cell Phone Laws in California and Elsewhere

Beginning July 1, anyone under age 18 will be prohibited from using a cell phone, laptop, PDA, pager or two-way messaging device while driving in California. Traffic officers, however, will not be allowed to pull over drivers simply because of a cell phone infraction. The fine for the first offense will be $20, and each additional violation will cost $50.

Similar laws are in effect in 15 other states (Colorado, Connecticut, Delaware, Illinois, Maine, Maryland, Minnesota, Nebraska, New Jersey, North Carolina, Rhode Island, Tennessee, Texas, Virginia and West Virginia), as well as Washington, D.C.

EIGHT

Tracking Technology Will Make Teens Safer Drivers

Ted Balaker

In the following viewpoint Ted Balaker looks at a University of Iowa study that proves that teen driving improves when an in-car camera, dubbed DriveCam, monitors teens' driving. DriveCam runs continually, and records and saves ten seconds before and after risky driving behavior that could lead to an accident, such as accelerating rapidly or breaking suddenly. Parents then receive regular reports on incidents that trigger a recording, so they can review them with their teenagers and teach them to be better drivers. The study found that those most prone to trigger a recording during the preliminary period saw a 72 percent drop in safety-related events after using DriveCam for the next two months. This data suggests that this tracking technology will reduce the number of automobile crashes and, ultimately, save teen lives.

Over the decades, driving has been getting much safer (as measured by declining highway fatality rates). But how can we make roads safer still?

Teenagers, especially boys, are (big surprise) some of the most dangerous drivers. Maybe we could yank their keys? Or just mount some cameras?

In-Car Cameras Can Change Driving Habits

There is a curve in the road near Alexander Mougin's house near Oxford, Iowa. The high-school senior used to like to take it hard and sharp—but that was before his car was fitted with a camera capable of recording his driving habits.

Mr. Mougin, 18 years old, has been participating in a University of Iowa study to see whether the device and the data it provides can help improve teen driving. The camera, attached to the rear-view mirror, has one lens facing the road and another aimed at the driver. It runs constantly, and slips into recording mode if, for example, the car accelerates rapidly or brakes suddenly. It then preserves about 10 seconds before and after the event that triggered it.

Many car insurance companies have programs where in-car cameras monitor teen driving habits in an effort to reduce accidents involving teen mototrists.

"You don't want to set it off," Mr. Mougin says. After 10 months of taking part in the study, he says, "I know I'm a safer driver."

DriveCam Offered by Insurance Company

American Family Mutual Insurance Co., the nation's 10th largest car insurer, will offer some of its customers the same system, known as DriveCam, in an effort to improve driving behavior among teens, a population that is particularly at risk on the roads. More teenagers die in car crashes than from any other single cause.

Fatalities in Crashes Involving Young Drivers (Ages 15–20), 2005

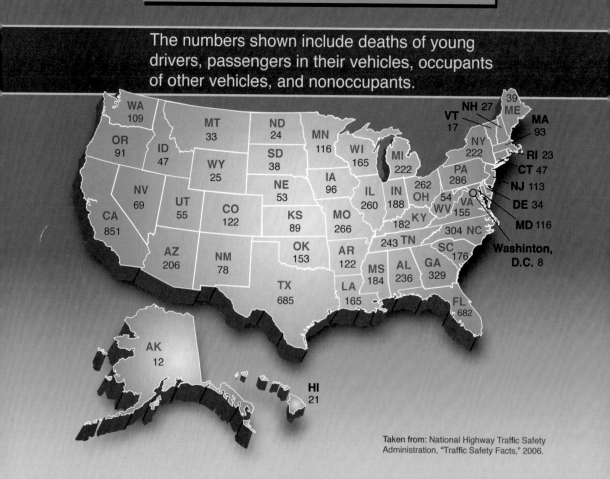

The numbers shown include deaths of young drivers, passengers in their vehicles, occupants of other vehicles, and nonoccupants.

WA 109
OR 91
ID 47
MT 33
ND 24
MN 116
WI 165
MI 222
NH 27
VT 17
ME 39
MA 93
NY 222
PA 286
RI 23
CT 47
NJ 113
NV 69
UT 55
WY 25
SD 38
NE 53
IA 96
IL 260
IN 188
OH 262
WV 54
VA 155
DE 34
MD 116
CA 851
AZ 206
CO 122
KS 89
MO 266
KY 182
TN 243
NC 304
Washinton, D.C. 8
NM 78
OK 153
AR 122
MS 184
AL 236
GA 329
SC 176
TX 685
LA 165
FL 682
AK 12
HI 21

Taken from: National Highway Traffic Safety Administration, "Traffic Safety Facts," 2006.

Customers with teenage children in Indiana, Minnesota and Wisconsin will be able to request that the system be installed in their cars, free of charge. Parents will receive regular reports on incidents that trigger a recording, which they can then review with their kids.

The system, made by DriveCam Inc., a privately held firm in San Diego, is the latest in a line of tools that can help parents track their teenagers' behavior.

Study Shows In-Car Cameras Reduce Risky Driving

The company says it won't watch the videos, but you can bet Mom and Dad will. And often that's often enough to provoke safer driving habits:

The Iowa study includes 25 teenagers who have driven 300,000 total miles in 10 months. The researchers first let the teens drive with the device, but hid the light that lets a driver know the recording has been triggered. After several weeks, they uncovered the light, and began sending results to parents.

Those most prone to trigger a recording during the preliminary period saw a 72% drop in safety-related events after using DriveCam for the next two months, says Daniel McGehee, director of the Human Factors & Vehicle Safety Research division of the university's Public Policy Center.

The self-interested reasons for offering the free service: It's a great way to lure customers, and:

If the program reduces the number of crashes, that could contribute to lower insurance payouts. In 2005, the last year for which data are available, nearly 5,700 16-to-20 year olds died on the roads, according to the National Highway Traffic Safety Administration, about 13% of all crash deaths. Another 53,000 suffered incapacitating injuries.

NINE

Parental Consequences Deter Dangerous Teen Driving Behaviors

Students Against Destructive Decisions and Liberty Mutual Insurance Group

The following viewpoint describes the findings of a joint research project conducted by the insurance company Liberty Mutual Group and SADD, Inc. (Students Against Destructive Decisions). After reviewing the data, the authors conclude that parental consequences significantly deter dangerous driving behaviors—such as driving while drunk or high—in teens. The project focused on a survey of 903 teens with a driver's license from a national sample of twenty-six high schools in April and May 2006. According to the authors, parents affect teen driving behaviors by setting clear expectations and following through with consequences when rules are not followed.

One in five teens is still drinking and driving, and one in nearly eight teens is still using marijuana and driving. That's according to the seventh annual *Teens Today* driving study . . . released [in September 2006] by Liberty Mutual and SADD (Students Against Destructive Decisions). But parents who set clear consequences—and follow through on them— significantly reduce the likelihood that their teen will engage in these and other unsafe behaviors behind the wheel.

Students Against Destructive Decisions and Liberty Mutual Insurance Group, "New Study: Parental Consequences Significantly Deter Dangerous Behaviors in Teens," September 2006. Reproduced by permission.

These driving results are part of *Teens Today*, an annual multi-part research study that reports on teens' behaviors, attitudes, and decision-making about issues such as driving, drinking, drug use, sexual activity, and family/peer relationships.

Parental Expectations Reduce Dangerous Behaviors

Overall, 19 percent of teens report driving under the influence of alcohol, 15 percent report driving under the influence of marijuana, and 7 percent report driving under the influence of "other drugs." But teens say parents who set expectations with clear consequences for them about breaking the law while driving are less

Studies have shown that parents can profoundly impact a teen's decisions about safe driving when on the road.

likely to have driven under the influence of alcohol (16 percent vs. 29 percent), marijuana (14 percent vs. 18 percent), or other drugs (6 percent vs. 11 percent) than are teens whose parents do not set any consequences.

And, further, teens who have never driven under the influence of any illegal substance are a third more likely to say their parents will follow through with those consequences than are teens who have driven under the influence of either alcohol or marijuana (78 percent vs. 59 percent).

"It's quite encouraging to see that parental involvement can significantly improve teen driving statistics, a mission we've been committed to for some time now," said Paul Condrin, Liberty Mutual president, Personal Market. "And through this study, the type of parental involvement that works is clear—parents need to know the laws and teen-driving rules of their state, set clear expectations with their teens about what safe driving is, and establish and enforce those consequences should those laws be broken or expectations not be met."

Parents Must Follow Through on Consequences

The study finds that setting expectations and following through on consequences may help prevent teens from getting into car crashes, which are the leading cause of death for American teens—more than drugs, guns, or any disease combined. Establishing consequences also cuts down on the number of teens who engage in other unsafe driving behaviors:

- Teens whose parents establish clear consequences for breaking family driving rules are less likely to drive more than 5 mph over the speed limit (44 percent) than are teens whose parents do not set consequences (56 percent).
- Teens whose parents establish clear consequences for breaking family driving rules are less likely to drive with three or more passengers in a car (36 percent vs. 42 percent) or eat or drink while driving (31 percent vs. 40 percent) than are their counterparts who do not have any clear consequences set.

- Interestingly, simply establishing consequences about talking on the cell phone while driving does not significantly influence behavior. However, teens who say their parents are likely to enforce any established consequences for breaking their family driving rule about cell phones are significantly less likely to talk on the cell phone while driving (37 percent) than are teens who say their parents are unlikely to actually follow through on any consequence (65 percent).

Some Parents Hold Back on Guidance

In many instances, parents are actually present while teens engage in risky driving habits. Even when adults are in the car with teens, the Liberty Mutual/SADD study shows that teens engage in bad driving choices, such as speeding (almost 50 percent of the time), talking on their cell phones (about 20 percent of the time), and eating or drinking while driving (almost 20 percent of the time).

"Parents can play an incredibly influential role in the driving behavior of their teens," said Stephen Wallace, chairman and chief executive officer of the national SADD organization. "Perhaps most important is to set a good example for young drivers and to reinforce their good driving habits by praising what they are doing right behind the wheel."

Boys Are at Greater Risk

The Liberty Mutual/SADD driving study also found that boys are more likely than girls to have driven under the influence of alcohol, marijuana, and other drugs (32 percent vs. 25 percent), yet boys say their parents are less likely to speak to them about driving safely. In addition, parents are establishing fewest consequences for their teenage boys when it comes to this behavior.

"Older teen boys are more likely than girls to engage in bad driving choices while adults are present," said Condrin. "While it's important to talk to both teenage girls and boys about safe driving, parents should remember that boys are more at risk these days for destructive driving."

Parents Need to Model Good Driving Behaviors

71% of parents admit they have talked on a cell phone while their teens were in the car.

62% of parents admit they have operated a radio, MP3 player, game, or other device while driving.

25% of parents admit they have broken a law while driving with their teen in the car (running a red light or stop sign, illegal U-turn, etc.).

Taken from: Allstate Insurance Company, "Smart Parent Involvement Key in Preventing Teen Driving Deaths," 2007. http://media.allstate.com/releases/2304-smart-parent-involvement-key.

What Parents Can Do

"While young people across the country have done a remarkable job of helping to reduce alcohol-related crash deaths among their peers by almost 60 percent since 1981, this new data makes clear that their work is not done," said Wallace. "Too many teens continue to drink and drug and drive, and parents must be relentless in talking to their teens about this important issue."

The seventh annual *Teens Today* driving study builds upon six years of previous research. Experts on teen driving behaviors, Liberty Mutual and SADD offer these additional tips to help parents talk to their teens.

- Know your state's Graduated Driver License law, including restrictions on supervised driving, time of day, and passengers in the car and enforce them.
- Set family rules about driving, outline clear consequences for breaking the rules, and follow through. Liberty Mutual

and SADD suggest some rules, if they are not covered by your state laws:

- No friends in the car without an adult;
- No driving after 10 p.m.;
- No use of alcohol or other drugs;
- No distractions while driving including eating, changing CDs, handling iPods and putting on makeup; and
- No cell phone use, including text messaging.

- Start talking with children as young as 13 or 14 about driving and driving safety. From focus groups, Liberty Mutual and SADD have learned from parents of teen drivers that the best times to talk with teens about driving safety are during the 1–2 years before they get their license.
- Continue supervised driving once your child has received his or her license and reinforce the rules and safe driving habits.
- Don't relent. Parents should continue the dialogue with their teens and frequently reinforce the acute dangers of drinking and driving or using drugs and driving.

Parent-Teen Driving Contracts Deter Dangerous Driving Behaviors

J.M. White and W.E. Van Tassel

In the following viewpoint J.M. White and W.E. Van Tassel examine parent-teen driving agreements, describing what they are and how they should be written. The key factor in their success, according to the authors, is setting clear rules and regulations along with consequences for breaking the agreement. The authors list a variety of behaviors, such as meeting curfews and maintaining good grades in school, that should be included in the contract to help teens become more responsible. The authors assert that vehicle care and maintenance are also an important part of the parent-teen driving agreement. White and Van Tassel work in Driver Training Operations at the American Automobile Association (AAA) national office.

Parent-Teen Driving Agreements are just one way for parents to play an active role in developing safe teen drivers. The Parent-Teen Driving Agreement is a contractual arrangement between parents and teens that states the rules and regulations for driving and the consequences for contractual violations. This article, which identifies and explores the importance of teen responsibili-

J.M. White and W.E. Van Tassel, "Parent-Teen Driving Agreements: Contracts for Safety?" American Driver and Safety Education Association, 2007. Reproduced by permission.

ties and behaviors in Parent-Teen Driving Agreements, is part of a series of articles that will examine the components for promoting parent and teen responsibilities and safe behaviors, and how to use a Parent-Teen Driving Agreement to its full potential.

Parent-Teen Driving Agreements Set Rules and Regulations

One of the biggest challenges of parenthood occurs when children become novice drivers. There are many ways for parents to play an active role in this teenage milestone, and developing a Parent-Teen Driving Agreement is just one of the ways. With motor vehicle crashes being the leading cause of death in people ages 3 to 34 and with an estimated 5,000 teenagers dying in automobile crashes every year, developing a Parent-Teen Driving Agreement may make the difference between life and death. But what is a Parent-Teen Driving Agreement?

A Parent-Teen Driving Agreement is an agreement between teens and their parents, regarding driving privileges and the use of motor vehicles. These agreements typically set forth the rules and regulations as well as the agreed consequences of violating the agreement. Not only the teen must commit to this agreement, but the parents must as well. It is important to establish that both parent and teen are entering into a contract together and that both have a voice in the contract. More importantly, the parents must also follow certain rules and regulations in order for the contract to work to its full potential. Leading by example is the foundation of such a contract and parents must commit to this leadership role. It is the goal of this . . . article to discuss the roles that both the parent and teen play in the contract and to identify what they must do in order for it to be successful.

This article will focus on what components are related to the teen driver and how feedback provided during scheduled meetings between parents and teen(s) can enhance driver performance. Two main components will be presented and further broken down into areas of responsibility: driver behavior and vehicle maintenance. Additionally, consequences for vehicle misuse and

A Parent-Teen Driving Agreement is an agreement between teens and their parents regarding the use of the car and driving privileges.

negative behaviors are presented since the teen and parent must agree to the terms and conditions for violating the contractual agreement.

Important Teen Behaviors Should Be Identified

It is important to identify what types of behaviors are expected of the teen related to safe vehicle operation. The teen is responsible for following the behaviors identified by the contract and fully understanding what is expected of him or her. Operating a motor vehicle demands respect and the teen must be held accountable for his/her behavior at all times.

There are many behaviors that a teen should display while driving and some of the critical behaviors are:

- using safety belts;
- obeying traffic laws;
- and reducing distractions.

While most teen drivers have completed some sort of driver's education program, it is still important to make sure that the behaviors learned in class are continually assessed, and the Parent-Teen Agreement is a good way to do this. The contract can target the behaviors that are most critical to safe driving and continually assess teen driver performance through periodic meetings between the parent and teen. The behaviors listed above are just some of the ones that are critical to maintaining safe and responsible teen driving. These behaviors are examined in greater detail.

Safe Driving Practices Explained

The U.S. Department of Transportation reported that in 2003, safety belts saved more than 14,903 American lives. However, during that same year, nearly two-thirds (60 percent) of passenger vehicle occupants killed in traffic crashes were not wearing a safety belt. Driving research has shown that lap/shoulder belts, when used properly, reduce the risk of fatal injury to front-seat passenger car occupants by 45 percent and the risk of moderate to critical injury by 50 percent. For light truck occupants, safety belts reduce the risk of fatal injury by 60 percent and moderate-to-critical injury by 65 percent. These are some powerful reasons as to the importance of safety belt use. It is up to the teen to follow the safety belt policy outlined in the Parent-Teen Agreement and make the right choice to mandate that s/he and all passengers will wear safety belts at all times to reduce risk.

Road engineers know the road better than anyone else and they recommend speed limits based on a variety of complex factors. It is best practice to follow and respect posted speed limits. However, it's also important for the teen to understand that they must not only obey speed limits, but also be aware of factors that affect their speed. Visibility, surface conditions and traffic are just three factors that a teen should keep in mind when driving at all times. Being aware of the factors that affect speed and effectively adjusting speed are critical to reducing risk.

Furthermore, the teen is responsible for obeying all traffic laws and to demonstrate that they know and respect the rules of the road. Not obeying traffic laws can have serious consequences and it's important that the teen be aware of how illegal or irresponsible behavior can result in devastating life-changing consequences. By stressing in the Parent-Teen Agreement the consequences associated with violating the law, teens will be cognizant of how important it is to maintain and demonstrate safe driving behaviors.

Safe Driver Behaviors Explained

While it may be impossible to control what is going on outside the vehicle, it is important to know that making certain decisions inside the vehicle can help reduce risk. By managing distractions inside the vehicle perception and judgment will be able to function optimally and attend to the most important task at hand, driving. In the contract, the teen will agree to avoid distractions inside the vehicle, and not participate in behaviors like:

- eating or drink in the car;
- using a cell phone while driving;
- or changing CDs.

Alcohol is the single largest cause of motor vehicles crashes, injuries and fatalities each year. Approximately 40 percent of all fatal crashes involve alcohol. That is why it's important to commit to not drive under the influence or ride with an impaired driver under any circumstance. It is important that the Parent-Teen Agreement stress the consequences of driving under the influence of alcohol, but also stress that other drugs, both legal (prescription and over-the-counter) and illegal (marijuana, ecstasy, or cocaine) can negatively affect driving behavior as well. By issuing a "zero-tolerance" rule in the contract stating that vehicle privileges will be taken away immediately should this rule be violated, teens will be more likely to avoid such dangerous behavior.

Additionally, the behaviors exhibited by the teen outside the vehicle play a critical role in being able to operate a sophisticated piece of machinery. It is important to incorporate into the contract behaviors that may not be directly related to driving a vehicle, but still affect the privilege of being able to do so. Some of the behaviors to incorporate into the Parent-Teen Agreement include, but are not limited to:

- school achievement;
- obeying driving curfew;
- maintaining open communication with parent for driving assistance and advice;
- and avoiding falling prey to peer pressure.

Driving Privileges Should Be Related to Positive Behaviors

As a new driver, it is easy to become distracted with the excitement of being able to drive. However, being able to drive should also be dependent on being able to maintain focus on education. If the contract states that driving privileges may be affected by school performance, it's then critical for the teen to maintain that performance. The Parent-Teen Agreement should state that strong academic performance yields additional driving privileges. Conversely, teens should be aware that poor academic performance yields a reduction or loss of driving privileges. This way the teen driver will work for what they want and maintain or in some cases improve their behavior in order to drive.

It is up to the teen to choose to exhibit the behaviors that will yield positive results. Setting a driving curfew is a way for the teen to demonstrate responsibility and respect for the driving privilege and Parent-Teen Agreement. The teen should be home at the time specified by the contract. However, should something come up, it is the responsibility of the teen to call his or her parents and explain the situation. The teen should fully understand the repercussions for failing to call and or missing curfew.

The teen should never be afraid to ask for driving advice or help. The contract should include that if the teen is in a difficult situation, that s/he will be able to rely on the support of the parent. Being able to ask parents for advice or help should never be intimidating or stressful. Therefore, no matter how difficult it may be, it is important to know and demonstrate responsible behaviors by seeking assistance when necessary.

Peer pressure may be one the greatest issues faced by teen drivers. However, it is important for the teen to exhibit strong resistance to peer pressure, especially when being pressured to perform risky driving behaviors. It is imperative that teen drivers exhibit maturity in decision making and avoid risk taking. The key is to always stay focused on driving safely and ensure the safety of all passengers, other drivers, and pedestrians. The Parent-Teen Agreement should act as a powerful reminder to the teen as to why it's important to avoid peer pressure. By being aware of the consequences of vehicle misuse, teens will be more likely to resist peer pressure and choose responsibility over recklessness.

Young Drivers Must Be Responsible for Vehicles

Besides demonstrating positive behaviors that influence driving, it's also important to know the responsibilities that come along with vehicle ownership. The Parent-Teen Agreement may set regulations and requirements that are centered on the vehicle itself. Some of these topics may include:
- which vehicles can be driven;
- vehicle maintenance;
- and financial responsibility.

The teen driver should know what vehicle(s) they are permitted to drive. For example, the Parent-Teen Agreement may specify that the teen driver can only operate vehicles with airbags. Additionally, it should specify which family vehicle(s) the teen is allowed to drive and which vehicles are off limits. It is the responsibility of the teen to follow the rules and regulations set forth by the contract and only drive the vehicle(s) the contract permits them to drive.

Driving comes with great responsibility. However, it is important that the teen not only be aware of the liability and health

"First Car," cartoon by Clive Goddard. www.Cartoonstock.com.

risk associated, but the financial responsibilities as well. The teen should know what they are responsible for and how to go about the process of caring for the vehicle. Two things that may be included in the Parent-Teen Agreement are engine maintenance and interior/exterior cleanliness.

Besides the financial responsibility associated with car care, there are other costs a teen should be aware of. Such costs include insurance, gas, vehicle registration, and parking decals. Most states require car insurance and it is the responsibility of the teen driver to understand their insurance and the importance of such a service and be prepared to contribute to this expense. Depending on the contract, some teens may be responsible for some or all of the costs mentioned above. The contract may use these additional costs as a way to teach teen drivers about the financial responsibility associated with vehicle ownership and operation.

Violating the Parent-Teen Driving Agreement Must Have Consequences

Should the teen violate the agreement set forth by the Parent-Teen Agreement, the teen should be aware of all consequences. For example, if the teen violates a rule or regulation, they may be faced with losing driving privileges for a certain amount of days, weeks, or even months. Another possible repercussion may be that the amount of miles a teen is allowed to drive weekly be decreased or the teen may face restrictions in the number of passengers they are allowed to have or they may have to pick up some extra household chores.

Should the teen not be responsible for their own insurance or gas, another repercussion to violating the contract may be taking over one, or both of the financial responsibilities. If a teen receives a ticket, s/he must be aware of both the legal consequences, financial consequences and the Parent-Teen consequences. However, the contract may also reward good behavior. Teens who exhibit strong, mature and respectful driving performance may receive positive feedback in the form of an increase in driving privileges. Feedback is the best way to reinforce behavior and is especially important when learning the complex task of driving.

Hopefully, this article has provided useful information regarding the role of the teen in the Parent-Teen Agreement. The goal of the contractual agreement isn't to make teen driving life difficult, but to help reinforce that driving is a dangerous and risky privilege and it must be respected and treated with maturity.

ELEVEN

The Right Car Makes Teens Safer on the Road

Jayne O'Donnell

Jayne O'Donnell is an auto writer at *USA Today*, specializing in car safety. In the following selection she concludes that size, power, and high-tech safety features make the difference in providing the safest cars for young drivers. O'Donnell consults various experts in highway traffic safety, examining some of the safest cars on the road today. According to O'Donnell, experts suggest that parents make safety—not appearance or performance—the number-one priority when buying a car for their teenage kids.

Sure, they're more likely to wreck the family car than any other member of your brood, but that's precisely why the teen drivers in the house need to be driving the safest car, which likely means a newer model.

Teens Should Drive the Best Family Car

What?!? It may seem counterintuitive, not to mention costly, but the argument for the "good" car going to the teen driver makes the most safety sense.

"If parents can afford a new vehicle, they should get one because newer vehicles tend to be safer in terms of crashworthiness and they're more likely to have important safety equipment such as side airbags," said Anne McCartt, senior vice president for research at the Insurance Institute for Highway Safety (IIHS).

After all, teen drivers are far more likely to have a fatal crash than adults. When they do crash, they are the most likely to have single-vehicle, run-off-the-road crashes, which often involve rollovers. That means they're the ones who *really* need stability control and side curtain airbags.

Comparison of Driver Traffic Fatalities by Size of Vehicle

Driver deaths per million registered passenger vehicles 1–3 years old, 2005

Vehicle Size	Rate
Car — Mini	144
Car — Small	106
Car — Midsize	70
Car — Large	67
Car — Very large	44
Pickup — Small	122
Pickup — Large	104
Pickup — Very large	101
SUV — Small	60
SUV — Midsize	57
SUV — Large	48
SUV — Very large	24

Taken from: Insurance Institute for Highway Safety, "Crash Fatalities," 2005.

"Vehicle choice does matter," said J. Peter Kissinger, president and CEO of the AAA [American Automobile Association] Foundation for Traffic Safety. "So discuss it in a serious way. Use it as another means to have a conversation with your teen."

The Right Car Saves a Teen's Life in a Crash

That's exactly what happened in the home of Dr. Art Kellerman, a professor who chairs the Department of Emergency Medicine at Atlanta's Emory University. He had seen the ramifications of bad vehicle choices too many times in his emergency room to let his 17-year-old son get the kind of car he wanted. The pair sat down with their lists of priorities. His son wanted power, looks and a good sound system. Dad wanted "safety, safety, reliability and economy."

Fortunately, Dad won, and the two agreed on a four-cylinder Honda Accord with side airbags and curtains. His only concession was a coupe to appeal to his son's styling preferences. A year after he bought the car, his son was T-boned at high speed at an intersection with a blind curve. Both the side bags and curtains deployed, preventing brain and other injuries, Kellerman says.

"That was the best money I ever spent," says Kellerman. "You can always buy another car, but you can't buy another kid."

Of course, this doesn't mean we're suggesting you hand over the keys to the BMW 7 Series or the Range Rover either. When it comes to the safest cars, there are three key things to consider for your teen driver.

Size Means Safety in a Car

It's true for all of us. It's especially true for young people, though— a mid- or larger-size car could be the difference between life and death in a crash.

"Don't buy the argument that you need something highly maneuverable and small," says Kissinger. "You simply don't have the skills to do that when you're a teenager."

Besides, there's no evidence that small cars make up in agility what they lack in size. You don't have to look any further than the April [2007] IIHS report on driver death rates for proof. The list of 16 models with the highest rates includes 11 small cars.

Former National Highway Traffic Safety Administration (NHTSA) chief Jeffrey Runge, a former emergency room physician, recommended vehicles weighing at least 3,300 pounds for teen drivers. That rules out compact cars and most small models and is a good general rule when choosing what class of vehicle to shop in. Some good choices for teen drivers, like some versions of the Toyota Camry or Honda Accord, weigh in slightly under 3,300 but still shouldn't be ruled out.

Small Cars Don't Protect Well in a Crash

Keep in mind that even a small car that earns five stars in most crash tests is only being judged in how well it protects in a crash with a similar-size vehicle. "A bigger vehicle protects in any type of crash," says McCartt. "The mantra for teens is big and boring."

State Farm Insurance has found that more than a third of teen drivers are in subcompact or compact cars and that drivers 20 or older were only half as likely to be in these very small vehicles. That's a mistake, says Kissinger. "You want a car that isn't so small they're going to automatically lose if they get into a crash, especially if they hit a larger vehicle."

Big, yes, but SUVs are generally not a good idea for teens, most safety experts say. Although these light trucks have low death rates as a group, they can also be difficult for anyone to handle in emergencies—they are required to carry a label on the visor warning that "abrupt maneuvers" should be avoided. "As a general rule I don't think SUVs are a great idea when learning to drive—and certainly not an older SUV that doesn't have ESC (electronic stability control) and tends to roll over," says Kissinger.

Speed Kills in a Crash

All of that could suggest to some that the Big Bimmer would be perfect. Not so fast. The second key to choosing the right car is remembering that a lot of horsepower can be a deadly temptation for a teen. Teens are the most likely to take risks behind the wheel so the last thing a car should do is encourage *more* risk-taking.

"If you have a choice, choose one that has less power than a sporty version," says Kissinger. Indeed, the IIHS's recent report on vehicle death rates not only found that small cars had the highest death toll, it found that among small cars, sporty cars had the highest death toll. Three sports cars—including the Ford Mustang—and several sporty cars, including the Acura RSX and Pontiac Sunfire, were on the list.

AAA recommends parents rule out both the quickest and slowest vehicle as unsafe—the latter could actually cause problems by being too pokey during lane changes or highway merges. Jack Peet, manager of community safety services for AAA Michigan, says vehicles that accelerate from zero to 60 mph in anywhere

Newer, larger vehicles are most likely to have lifesaving devices, such as airbags, that make them safer for teen drivers.

from eight to 11 seconds are safe bets for teens. Many car lovers will find that anathema to everything they stand for, but it's not a bad rule of thumb. Hey, a four-cylinder Toyota Camry will still get them where they're going!

"In the old days it was pretty easy: Everybody recommended getting a 240 Volvo," says Kissinger. "Now there are a lot more choices, but you still want a run-of-the-mill boring car—which is a problem, because that's not what teens want to drive."

Check Crash Test Scores Before Buying a Car

As when choosing any car, it's wise to check crash tests scores from the government and the IIHS. Go to the Edmunds Car Safety Guide to find the NHTSA's crash test results and check the IIHS site for its ratings and recommendations. As for equipment, getting a car equipped with driver and passenger airbags and antilock brakes should go without saying. Side airbags *and* side curtain airbags—which deploy down from the roof rail to protect the head—are highly recommended. And stability control, which becomes mandatory on all passenger vehicles by 2012, would be the best bet of all. It will help teen drivers avoid crashes, kicking in with braking and engine power if the system senses the driver is losing control of the vehicle—a highly likely scenario.

If there's still money in your teen car budget after all of this, it pays to consider some of the more advanced crash-avoidance technologies showing up on new models. Check out, in particular, the emergency brake assist, lane departure and blind spot warnings mentioned in "Top 10 High-Tech Car Safety Technologies."

While it's common to seek out a used car for a teen driver, keep in mind that a vehicle more than three or four years old is pretty unlikely to have the latest safety equipment. Only in the last three years have many non-luxury cars had stability control or side airbags available. But if you're lucky enough to find an affordable slightly older model with the right features, go for it.

When it comes to car shopping for a teen driver, Kellerman sums it up well: "If you can't afford the safest car, buy the safest car you can afford."

TWELVE

The Spread of Drag Racing Leads to Teenage Deaths

Sara B. Miller

Sara B. Miller, staff writer for the *Christian Science Monitor*, explores the growth of teenage drag racing, not just in California, but in Massachusetts as well. She links street racing's growing popularity to its glorification in movies such as *American Graffiti* and *The Fast and the Furious*, and states that even if teenagers are not racing, speeding may still be an issue. The politics surrounding driving restrictions for teenagers make it difficult for legislators to raise the driving age or make graduated licensing laws all encompassing. The San Diego Police Department created a full-time unit called Dragnet, which sanctions races at a local stadium, but this program is highly controversial because some say it encourages teens to drive too fast and gives them a false sense of security. Captain Michael Murphy of the Revere [Massachusetts] Police Department says it is important for teenagers to realize that "they are not nearly the accomplished drivers that they think they are."

Young street racers have been drawn to a straight swath of Lynn Marsh Road in Revere, Mass., for as long as Capt. Michael Murphy of the Revere Police Department can remember.

But . . . what was once possibly a casual race with a few kids has grown into a more sophisticated spectacle. He says some of the characteristics of races in California, long the cradle of America's street racing set, glorified in "The Fast and the Furious" movies, have found their way East.

Statistics from the Massachusetts Registry of Motor Vehicles reveal that citations for drag racing increased from 510 in 2002 to 578 [in 2004].

"It has crept our way," Captain Murphy says.

Now officials want that to change. Recently in Massachusetts, in a two-week period alone, two deadly crashes among teens—one involving high speed late at night, the other an apparent drag race—have cut five lives short.

High-Speed Driving Leads to Teen Deaths

The accidents come as lawmakers seek to rein in teen driving rights in an effort to cut down on crashes. The legislation mirrors action in statehouses across the country, as parents, police, and politicians grapple with an accident rate per mile for teens that is four times that of older drivers.

Officials say inexperience behind the wheel often plays a role, but so does risky behavior and bad judgment. The number of fatalities of teens involving speed—including driving too fast for conditions, in excess of the limit, or racing—has crept up in recent years. Forty-five percent of fatalities for teen drivers ages 16 to 20 involved speed in 2003, up from 43 percent in 1999, according to the National Highway Traffic Safety Administration.

"What the safety community is seeing now is that we made gains in seat belt use and in drunk driving, but those gains are being offset by lack of progress on speeding . . . which is particularly a problem with young males," says Barbara Harsha, the executive director of the Governors Highway Safety Association.

Street racing was glorified in 1973 with George Lucas's "American Graffiti" and in 2001 with "The Fast and the Furious" and its 2003 sequel. But long after premieres and box office tallies have come and gone, officials across the country continue to wage

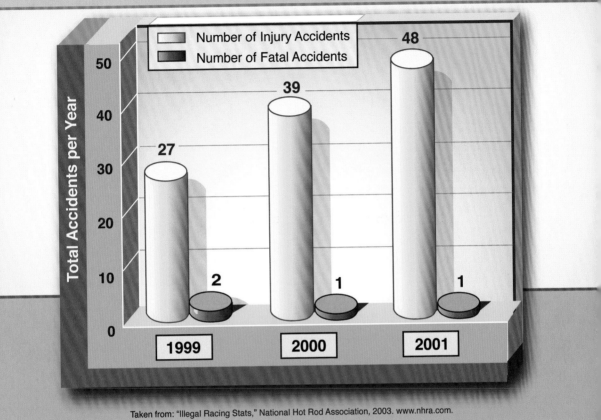

Street Racing Accidents in Florida

As Reported by the Florida Department of Highway and Safety for Motor Vehicles

- Number of Injury Accidents
- Number of Fatal Accidents

Total Accidents per Year

50 — 40 — 30 — 20 — 10 — 0

1999: 27, 2

2000: 39, 1

2001: 48, 1

Taken from: "Illegal Racing Stats," National Hot Rod Association, 2003. www.nhra.com.

war against the love for speed, the chase, and a rush of adrenaline. Teens are not the only ones who participate in street racing, and racing is just one factor—including speeding, drinking, and error —in teen fatalities each year.

Legislative Action

Lawmakers in Massachusetts want to fight these factors with a bill that would extend teen training periods in class and behind the

Teenagers who participate in drag racing may enjoy the rush of excitement in beating their opponents on the open road, but they do not fully understand the consequences of accidental deaths and injuries that they can inflict on themselves and others.

wheel with a supervisor, and give police greater power to enforce curfew and passenger restrictions.

While almost all states have some sort of graduated licensing system in place, their rules vary greatly, says Russ Rader, a spokesperson for the Insurance Institute for Highway Safety. Recently, many have gotten tougher: setting driving curfews earlier or barring teens from using cell-phones while driving.

To the backdrop of the legislative movement is a debate on whether to raise the driving age limit altogether, says Ms. Harsha. But that debate hasn't gone very far, partly because many parents balk at the idea of two extra years of chauffeuring their children. "It's a very political issue, particularly in farm states," she says.

Some places have taken steps to control racing, rather than eradicate it. Take San Diego: One Friday night in September 2001, patrol officers tallied all the cars gathered at a local drag racing spot. They counted 1,200.

"Patrol officers were busy writing tickets, but it was not having an impact. The problem was getting bigger," says John Austin, a detective at the San Diego Police Department.

Dragnet

With grant money, the department established a full-time unit called Dragnet whose sole purpose has been fighting drag racing. They also pushed the City Council to make watching drag races a crime and forfeiture of a car the possible punishment for racing. They steered drivers to a local stadium where races are sanctioned and legal on certain evenings.

So far, Detective Austin says, the program has worked. In 2002, there were 16 deaths directly related to street racing. [In 2004] there were none.

But while Austin says his unit hears from officials around the world seeking more information on their program, not everyone thinks that sanctioned racing is a good idea. "[Such programs] simply encourage teens to drive fast, and give them a false sense of security," says Mr. Rader. "What guarantee is there that they won't drive like that on streets?"

In Revere, Murphy says that even with increased patrols and tougher laws, the problem won't end without the cooperation of parents, who often watch blindly as their kids "soup up" their Honda Accords and Acuras.

"Even if we are successful [on Lynn Marsh Road], it will only send them somewhere else. . . . They are going to race, and they are going to crash, because they are not nearly the accomplished drivers that they think they are," he says. "They are kids."

THIRTEEN

Driving All-Terrain Vehicles Can Be Dangerous

Jeff Manning, Brent Walth, and Susan Goldsmith

> In the following selection Jeff Manning, Brent Walth, and Susan Goldsmith, writers for the Portland newspaper *Oregonian*, provide a comprehensive examination of the all-terrain vehicle (ATV) industry, safety laws, and accident statistics. The Consumer Product Safety Commission said child injuries have increased 18 percent overall on ATVs since 2001. Reasons for this include ATV design and improper usage. The *Oregonian*'s analysis found that 80 percent of ATV crashes are ones in which riders have ignored product safety warnings. However, the authors point out situations in which experienced ATV drivers have followed the rules but still lost their lives in ATV accidents.

The final weekend in March 2007 dawned gray and damp across much of the country—but eager riders pulled out their all-terrain vehicles anyway and hit the springtime trails.

Soon the ambulances rolled, too. In North Carolina, an ATV overturned and crushed an 18-year-old woman to death. A collision with a truck killed two ATV riders in Centertown, Ky. Two girls, ages 4 and 7, died in separate ATV wrecks in eastern Texas. And two infants—a 14-month-old in South Carolina and an 8-month-old in Perris, Calif.—died in two more ATV crashes. In Oregon that weekend, Debby Schubert, 45, and Donnie Moody, 31, became the state's first ATV fatalities in 2007 when their machine tumbled into a dry canal east of Redmond.

Nine dead, including four children. Another bloody weekend in ATV country, where the quest for thrills and family fun can turn to grief in one terrifying moment.

Nearly 20 years ago, the federal government declared ATVs an "imminent hazard" and forced manufacturers to drop unstable three-wheel models in favor of the four-wheelers sold today. Regulators also compelled the ATV industry to adopt safety warnings and offer rider training to stem the accidents.

Since then, federal officials have done little more than tally the dead, and the failure of their approach can be seen in the grim body counts from Oregon to West Virginia.

The rate of injuries per ATV has barely budged from where it stood in the years after the government acted in 1988. Though death rates initially plummeted as three-wheelers disappeared, there's been scant improvement since.

Over the past decade, the machines have soared in popularity, with 7.6 million in use. The result: Record numbers of riders end up in emergency rooms and morgues as accidents kill about 800 people a year and injure an estimated 136,700.

"This is one of the worst examples ever of a government agency failing in its fundamental mission to protect the American public," Stuart M. Statler, a former U.S. Consumer Product Safety Commission member, said of the agency's inability to significantly reduce ATV deaths and injuries during the past two decades.

Statler never imagined, when he helped lead the crackdown on ATVs in the 1980s, that deaths might someday surpass 1,000. Now, nearly 8,000 people have died in ATV crashes since the commission began counting, and 2 million have been seriously hurt.

A quarter of the dead and nearly a third of the injured are children. In Oregon, at least 82 people have died on ATVs since 2000, including 22 younger than 16. Serious ATV injuries in the state have increased at almost double the national rate in recent years.

Safety risks haven't dented the allure of ATVs. Over the past decade, sales tripled to $5 billion a year as companies introduced

The popularity of all-terrain vehicles has increased in the last decade. Accidents have increased, too; currently, 800 are killed and 136,700 are injured each year.

bigger, faster models. Though companies have added new features such as four-wheel drive and power steering, they haven't eliminated a long-standing problem: overturns. The machines flip over with punishing regularity—smashing faces, breaking necks, crushing chests.

The major manufacturers—Honda, Polaris, Yamaha, Kawasaki, Suzuki, Bombardier and Arctic Cat—insist their machines are safe and stable if operated properly. They fault riders for accidents.

"The safety issue is with the appropriate use," William Willen, a lawyer for ATV market leader Honda, told *The Oregonian.* "It's how people use the machines." Honda's safety slogan sums it up: "Stupid Hurts."

But reckless riders are only part of the problem. The federal government has not extensively tested ATV stability since at least 1991.

The newspaper analyzed fatal crashes and reached a surprising finding: Overturns were as common among riders who appeared to be obeying basic safety warnings as among those who didn't.

Together, the results point to the role that ATV design plays in many crashes, yet regulators have largely ignored it. Meanwhile, abundant evidence shows that riders don't follow the warnings and decline free training programs, the key tenets of the government and industry approach to safety.

The Riders

On a chilly weekend last August [2006], thousands of ATV riders flocked to the south coast near Reedsport for DuneFest, the wildest ATV party of the year at the Oregon Dunes National Recreation Area.

Riders roared by at 60 mph, doing doughnuts and jumping over huge dunes that can soar hundreds of feet. Dozens lined up to challenge Banshee Hill, one of the biggest and steepest inclines. A man with no helmet crested the summit pulling a wheelie—a preschooler clutching the ATV's handlebars in front.

Nearby stood a small wooden cross, where three weeks earlier a passer-by found 23-year-old Justin Miller. An expert rider from Yelm, Wash., Miller wrecked his Yamaha Raptor and suffocated under the 400-pound machine.

Since the first ATV casualty reports long ago, manufacturers have deflected questions about the design and safety of their product by pointing to reckless behavior by their customers. Places such as the dunes, the epicenter of Northwest ATV culture, help explain why the industry's emphasis on rider responsibility and the government's reliance on warning labels haven't worked.

Few rules apply at the dunes, and disregard for ATV safety warnings is widespread. Riders go without helmets and carry passengers. They do jumps and stunts and ride over the roughest terrain. Some drink and drive. Children commonly race around on adult-sized machines. All are behaviors that ATV owner's manuals and the Consumer Product Safety Commission warn against.

Accidents aren't limited to public recreational areas like the dunes. A growing number involve riders taking ATVs on paved roads, where traffic increases odds of a collision. Millions use them for ranching, hunting and family outings on private trails, and the casualties hit riders of all ages and experience levels.

The Rollovers

Federal records show that more than half of those who die on ATVs perish in crashes where the machines roll over sideways or flip forward or backward. In some cases, overturns happen after the ATV hits something or tumbles off a steep drop.

But about a third of the time, the government data show, rollovers are the first known event in a fatal crash. And as ATV companies make heavier machines, overturns pose an increasing danger. The Arctic Cat 500 that crushed an Oregon rider in 2006, for example, is among the heavier ATVs made—more than 600 pounds.

ATV companies are quick to point to the large number of crashes in which riders ignore warnings. That is true more than 80 percent of the time in the government's database of fatal crashes, *The Oregonian's* analysis found.

The warnings are posted right on the ATVs and state clearly what riders shouldn't do: drink and drive, ride without a helmet, carry a passenger or operate an adult machine if under 16. Labels also warn against riding on public roads, where traffic is a hazard, or on pavement, because ATV tires are for off-road surfaces.

But failure to comply with warnings doesn't always explain rollovers, *The Oregonian* found. Working with the Consumer Product Safety Commission's crash data, the newspaper examined 2,732 fatal accidents involving four-wheel ATVs since 2000 and separated the cases into two groups: the large group of riders who ignored at least one safety warning, and the much smaller group of riders who didn't.

The newspaper then looked to see how often overturns were the primary event in the crash. The unexpected result: Riders who followed the warnings overturned in about two out of five cases, a rate comparable to the frequency of rollovers in the group that ignored one or more warnings.

A lawyer for the industry's trade group, the Specialty Vehicle Institute of America, called *The Oregonian*'s analysis "fatally flawed," saying the industry's research over the years shows the benefits of following warnings.

ATV Design Flaws Cause Rollovers

The persistence of rollovers among riders who followed the basic precautions shows why engineers and safety advocates have long pointed to another factor: ATV design.

ATVs have a narrow track width and high ground clearance, necessary qualities that allow them to travel on rough territory and narrow trails. The same qualities make them far less stable than cars or SUVs.

Under pressure about rollovers, the ATV companies in 1988 signed agreements with the Consumer Product Safety Commission pledging not to build four-wheel ATVs with less sideways stability than those they sold at the time. Since 1991, the commission hasn't performed tests to check whether the companies kept their pledge.

To find out, the newspaper hired engineer Thomas R. Fries of Portland to measure the stability of four popular models. Fries has been a plaintiff's expert in ATV lawsuits and has done defense work in other vehicle crash cases.

Fries followed industry and Consumer Product Safety Commission methods. He first measured front and back stability— called pitch stability—and found that all four machines met the current, industry-adopted standard. But Fries said the government's test method overstates stability by 10 percent to 15 percent.

To get a more realistic result, he performed a different test. ATVs were placed on a table and tilted sideways to discover their tip angle—the point at which their upper wheels lift off the surface. The tilt table method is better, Fries said, because it accounts for the way an ATV's suspension and tires behave. On the tilt table test, all of the machines came in below a stability threshold Fries considered safe.

"They're dangerous," Fries said. "They are too prone to tipping over."

Small Changes in ATV Design Could Improve Stability

Fries said that small changes in ATV design—such as widening the track width by a couple of inches and lowering the rider seating position—would significantly increase stability. . . .

The ATV manufacturers don't dispute that their machines can roll or flip. Instead, they argue that ATVs are a special breed of vehicle they describe as "rider-active." In other words, it's up to drivers to keep the ATV upright by shifting their body weight from side to side or front to back.

State figures show that the number of ATV permits sold in Oregon doubled over six years, and so did the number of trauma cases, reaching 414 in 2005. That's twice the rate that injuries grew nationally in the same period.

The industry's trade group says the rising numbers of dead and injured simply reflect the fact that more ATVs are in use. "Millions of Americans operate ATVs safely every day," said Tim Buche, executive director of the Specialty Vehicle Institute of America.

Instead, the group focuses on the rate of injury per 10,000 ATVs, arguing that it has declined since 2001. The group also says children younger than 16 make up a smaller portion of the injured—30 percent—than a few years ago.

It is true that injury rates have shifted some since 2001, but according to the Consumer Product Safety Commission's latest report, the changes aren't significant enough to indicate a trend up or down.

Of the 136,700 people hurt seriously enough to be hospitalized in 2005, an estimated 40,400 were children. The commission said child injuries have increased 18 percent overall since 2001. The industry points to a 10 percent dip in child injuries [in 2004], but the commission says that change wasn't statistically significant.

ATV-Related Deaths and Injuries for Children Under Sixteen

Year	Reported Deaths	Percentage of Total Reported Deaths for All Ages	Estimated Number of Emergency-Room Treated Injuries	Percent of Estimated Injuries for All Ages
2005	*120*	*26*	*40,400*	*30*
2004	*155*	*25*	*44,700*	*33*
2003	*152*	*24*	*38,600*	*31*
2002	*133*	*25*	*37,100*	*33*
2001	132	26	34,300	31
2000	124	28	32,000	35
1999	90	23	27,700	34
1998	82	33	25,100	37
1997	79	33	20,600	39
1996	87	35	20,200	38
1995	64	32	19,300	37
1994	54	27	21,400	42
1993	59	32	17,900	36
1992	71	32	22,000	38
1991	68	30	22,500	39
1990	81	35	22,400	38

Death data collection for 2002 and forward is incomplete and is denoted by italics. The percentages shown in column 3 for the years where reporting is incomplete should be interpreted with caution because the rate at which deaths are reported may not be consistent across all age groups.

Fatality trends are harder to characterize because the consumer agency has used different counting methods over the years. But except for an upward spike in 1999, when the newest method took effect, the agency's estimated risk of death has fluctuated little.

The commission disagrees with the industry's emphasis on rates. "Our commitment is to drive down not a rate of deaths and injuries," said commission spokesman Scott Wolfson, "but the numbers of actual lives and family members affected by incidents that are happening across the country."

Researchers Margie Gultry, Lynne Palombo and Kathleen Blythe of the Oregonian *contributed to this report.*

What You Should Know About Teen Driving

Facts About Teen Driving in the United States and Canada

- For every 100,000 teenage male drivers in the United States, 19.4 are killed in a driving fatality. American females are killed at the much lower rate of 11.1 per 100,000 drivers.
- The main causes of driver fatalities among male drivers between fifteen and twenty years of age in the United States are speeding (38 percent) and drinking and driving (24 percent).
- In the United States, fatal and nonfatal car crashes involving teen drivers cost an estimated $40.8 billion to the economy in 2002.
- Statistics broken down by age show that teens in the United States are the most at risk for crashes when they first begin driving: 16-year-old driver crash rates are three times those of 17-year-olds, five times those of 18-year-olds, and twice those of 85-year-olds.
- In Virginia, all teens under age eighteen must appear before a judge with their parents or legal guardians in order to receive their first driver's license. This is called a juvenile licensing ceremony.
- In their first year behind the wheel, 1 in 5 male 16-year-old drivers and about 1 in 10 female 16-year-old drivers in the United States will be involved in a crash.
- In 2001 Canadian drivers aged 16–19 years had a fatality rate that was four times that of drivers aged 25–34, and nine times that of drivers aged 45–54.

- For every billion vehicle kilometers traveled in Canada by drivers aged 16–19, there are 27 traffic fatalities. Drivers aged 25–34 reduce that rate to 6 fatalities per the same distance traveled, while the rate cuts in half again, to 3, for drivers between 45 and 54 years of age.
- Canadian drivers under the legal age of majority in their province or territory (18 or 19) require parental consent to obtain a learner's driving license.
- A study from Ontario, Canada, showed the graduated driver licensing program [GDL] for teen drivers was effective. Alcohol-related collisions declined 27 percent; collisions between midnight and 5 A.M. dropped 62 percent; and collisions on freeways were reduced by 61 percent.
- Crashes were not reduced in Ontario, Canada, among teen drivers who left their GDL program earlier after taking driver education classes. Instead, teen drivers who had earned certificates from approved driving schools had an overall collision rate 44 percent higher than novice drivers who had not earned a certificate.
- Three of Canada's thirteen provinces and territories require learners to display an L (Learner) sign/plate. This requirement is not in effect anywhere in the United States.

Facts About Driving Off-Road and Other Vehicles

- ATV injuries are the number one cause of sport- and recreation-related trauma injuries to youth under the age of nineteen in Canada.
- Kentucky reported the highest number of deaths in the United States involving ATVs in the period 2000–2005, with 143 deaths. It was followed by West Virginia (138), Pennsylvania (120), Florida (110), Tennessee (94), and Texas (87).
- The states reporting the fewest deaths involving ATVs between 2000 and 2005 were Rhode Island (2), Delaware (2), Vermont (7), Hawaii (8), and Connecticut (12).
- Between 1982 and 2005 in the United States, 2,178 children under the age of sixteen died in ATV incidents (30 percent of

the 7,188 total fatalities), with 917 of those children under the age of twelve.

- Young drivers using minibikes (off-road motorized bikes) suffered some ten thousand injuries between 2003 and 2004 in the United States.
- According to the U.S. Consumer Product Safety Commission, between 1998 and 2004, minibike accidents claimed forty-nine lives nationwide.
- Between 1990 and 2003, dirt bikes, minibikes, trail bikes, go-carts, mopeds, scooters, riding lawn mowers, golf carts, dune buggies, farm vehicles, snowmobiles, and boats resulted in more than 1.2 million U.S. hospital emergency room visits by children.
- Accidents among children using off-road and other motorized vehicles jumped 86 percent in the United States in thirteen years—the 1990 figure was 70,500, and the 2003 injuries numbered 130,900. Forty-eight percent of the injuries resulted from ATV use, but the other 52 percent of the injuries were due to other vehicle use.
- In the United States inexperience is the main cause of injury for young drivers operating personal watercraft. The majority of injuries are the result of running into objects like docks, other watercraft, or tree stumps.
- Boys under the age of sixteen are more than three times as likely as girls of the same age to be injured while driving snowmobiles.
- Of all snowmobilers treated in Ontario, Canada, emergency rooms, the largest group (16 percent) were fifteen- to nineteen-year-olds.

Facts About Driving Motorcycles

- U.S. statistics show that in motorcycle accidents the drivers are the most at-risk, accounting for 90 percent of those killed. Passenger fatalities have been constant at 10 percent over several years.
- Between 1996 and 2006, 90 percent of the motorcyclists killed in the United States were males.

- Motorcyclists in the United States are more likely to be killed in crashes involving more than one vehicle: 55 percent were killed in multivehicle crashes, while 45 percent were killed in single vehicle crashes.
- In the United States in 2005, 326 motorcycle operators aged 15 to 20 years old were killed, and an additional 9,000 were injured.
- In the United States, 45 percent of fatally injured motorcyclists did not wear helmets.
- In 1967 the U.S. government started requiring states to have universal helmet laws to qualify for federal highway funds. By 1975 all but three American states had helmet laws covering all motorcycle riders. Then, in 1976 Congress revoked the authority to impose the sanctions. Many states repealed or weakened their helmet laws.
- In 2000 Florida repealed its legal requirement for all motorcyclists to wear protective helmets. Helmet usage dropped from nearly 100 percent to just 50 percent, producing a 71 percent increase in fatalities and tripling the number of fatalities among drivers under twenty-one years of age. Florida now makes helmet use mandatory only for riders under age twenty-one and for older riders without at least $10,000 medical insurance.
- Motorcycle riders accounted for 11 percent of all national highway deaths in 2006, even though they are a small fraction of the total number of vehicles on the highway.
- According to a 2004 National Highway Traffic Safety Administration (NHTSA) study, motorcyclists are thirty-four times more likely to die on the highway than people riding in passenger cars.
- Mandatory helmet laws in Canada, along with the Canada Safety Council Course taken by about 85 percent of new motorcyclists, make it a world leader in motorcycle safety: between 1983 and 1999 motorcycle fatalities dropped 65 percent.
- The first motorcycle helmet use law in the world took effect on January 1, 1961, in Victoria, Australia.

What You Should Do About Teen Driving

An old proverb says, "Better a thousand times careful than once dead." The hard fact is that over 2.5 million people are injured in traffic accidents each year, and over forty-five thousand of those people die as a result. In reports released in 2008, statistics showed that drivers aged fifteen to twenty years accounted for 12.9 percent of all the drivers involved in fatal crashes and 16 percent of all the drivers involved in police-reported crashes. This record can be changed by careful driving.

Teens can be safer drivers—they can reduce the death toll on America's highways. Driver fatalities among fifteen- to twenty-year-olds increased by five percent between 1994 and 2004. Statistics consistently show that teens are nine times more likely to be in a car crash than are their parents. They also reveal that the crash rate increases 700 percent when teens are not driving with their parents.

Starting Out Safe

In early 2006 young drivers from fifty-four families in Minnesota and Wisconsin were enrolled in a Teen Safe Driver test project. After nine months in the program, these teens averaged a 70 percent decrease in the frequency and severity of high-risk driving events. During follow-up on the program, teens were surprised to see how often their actions contributed to risky events. At the moment of the event, they frequently attributed the problem to another driver's actions, but the video surveillance that formed an important part of the program objectively showed their contribution—being distracted, following too closely, or driving aggressively.

In addition to improving focus while driving, various factors have been identified on a worldwide basis that help reduce death and injury to young drivers. One of the first is seat belts, which should be worn by everyone in the vehicle—drivers and passengers. Sixty-three percent of fatally injured sixteen- to twenty-year-old passenger vehicle occupants were not wearing seat belts.

Graduated driver license (GDL) laws—which mandate that teens earn driver privileges in stages with restrictions gradually lifted as drivers gain experience—are one way to implement the safest driving practices that have been identified by researchers. However, it takes years for GDL laws to come into effect through the numerous development stages required in each state. Teens and their parents do not have to wait that long. They can examine the research and GDL laws of other states and countries for themselves and make their own driving agreements. Teen-parent driving agreements are contracts spelling out the driving rules and responsibilities for both the teens and the parents and also indicating the consequences if the rules are violated.

Practice Safe Driving Habits

Research shows that accidents involving teen drivers often have various common factors. During 2003 in the United States, a teen died in a traffic crash an average of once every hour on weekends. One of the reasons for this statistic is that weekends provide leisure time and opportunities to have fun with friends. Research around the world consistently proves that the more occupants there are in a car driven by a teen, the more likely the driver will be distracted and an accident may occur. In 2000, 63 percent of the deaths of thirteen- to nineteen-year-old passengers occurred when other teenagers were driving. GDL limits the number of passengers a teen driver can have in a car; so can teen-parent agreements.

Another reason for a high death rate on weekends is the consumption of alcohol by teen drivers. In the latest released statistics, 31 percent of drivers aged fifteen to twenty who were killed in motor vehicle crashes had been drinking. Each state has a legal alcohol limit that should never be exceeded, and most GDL laws enforce a much lower level or have zero tolerance for alcohol or drug use, a policy that is certainly the safest for all drivers.

Young drivers can also focus on avoiding distractions that cause accidents. A survey conducted with young drivers revealed many of them engage in risky behaviors behind the wheel. More than half (56 percent) of young drivers use cell phones while driving. Sixty-nine percent said that they speed to keep up with traffic and 64 percent said they speed to go through a yellow light. Forty-seven percent said that passengers sometimes distract them. Driving requires complete focus and attention at all times.

The Cost of Safety

Many of the things that can help teens become safer drivers cost money. Providing a teen driver with a new, safer car may just not be an option for many families. If teens must drive an older car, however, parents must make sure that it is mechanically sound before it leaves the driveway. Furthermore, installing monitoring equipment in a teen's vehicle can be a great asset in helping a teen see his or her own driving errors, and it provides parents with information on how their teen drives, but it is not something every family can afford. Instead, teens may need to spend many of their first driving miles supervised by a parent who can provide feedback on what to do in challenging situations.

Driver's education programs are not free to all teens but may be well worth the investment. Teens may contribute to the costs if they have part-time jobs, considering how important driving safely is to their futures. Even without a driver training program or parent available to spend time in the vehicle with them, teen drivers can keep a written log of every mile they drive and under what conditions. The log will help both parents and teens become aware of situations that may be riskier and help with planning driving experiences. Each mile of safe driving experience makes a teen a safer driver.

Advocates for Highway and Auto Safety
750 First St. NE, Ste. 901, Washington, DC 20002
(202) 408-1711 • fax: (202) 408-1699
e-mail: advocates@saferoads.org
Web site: www.saferoads.org

Advocates for Highway and Auto Safety is an alliance of consumer groups, health and safety groups, and insurance companies that seek to make America's roads safer. The alliance advocates the adoption of federal and state laws, policies, and programs that save lives and reduce injuries. On its Web site the organization publishes fact sheets, press releases, polls, and reports as well as links to legislative reports and testimony on federal legislation involving traffic safety, including issues surrounding teen driving.

American Driver & Traffic Safety Education Association (ADTSEA)
Highway Safety Center, Indiana University of Pennsylvania, R & P Bldg., Indiana, PA 15705
(724) 357-3975 • fax: (724) 357-7595
e-mail: support@hsc.iup.edu
Web site: http://adtsea.iup.edu

ADTSEA works with driver's education instructors and state authorities to improve driver's education standards and practices. On its Web site ADTSEA publishes white papers, articles, and reports, including *Brain Development and Risk-Taking in Adolescent Drivers, Suggested Standards for the Improvement of Driver Education,* and *Parent-Teen Driving Agreements: Contracts for Safety?*

Association for Safe International Road Travel (ASIRT)
11769 Gainsborough Rd., Potomac, MD 20854
(301) 983-5252

e-mail: asirt@asirt.org
Web site: www.asirt.org

ASIRT is a nonprofit, humanitarian organization that promotes road travel safety through education and advocacy. ASIRT provides travelers with road safety information, enabling them to make informed travel choices. ASIRT serves as a resource to governments, corporations, travel organizations, guidebooks, study abroad programs, health/travel clinics, and nongovernmental organizations. The organization also helps foster the development of new road safety organizations in other countries. ASIRT's publications include fact sheets, brochures, and the *ASIRT Newsletter*.

ATV Safety Institute (ASI)
2 Jenner, Ste. 150, Irvine, CA 92618-3806
(949) 727-3727
Web site: www.atvsafety.org

The ASI is a nonprofit division of the Specialty Vehicle Institute of America (SVIA) that provides all-terrain vehicle (ATV) safety education. Its primary goal is to promote the safe and responsible use of ATVs, thereby reducing accidents and injuries that may result from improper ATV operation. The ASI Web site offers press releases, information sheets, and pubic service announcements.

Concerned Families for ATV Safety
Web site: www.atvsafetynet.org

Concerned Families for ATV Safety is a network of parents dedicated to reducing injuries and death among children driving all-terrain vehicles. They offer support to victims' families and provide families with information and resources to make informed decisions about their children and ATVs. They work to raise awareness, through public education, of the need for adequate, common-sense safety standards; the organization promotes the idea that children under sixteen should not be driving ATVs and encourages the enforcement of ATV laws. The Web site provides studies, news releases, and personal stories about ATV safety.

4-H ATV Safety Program
National 4-H Council
7100 Connecticut Ave., Chevy Chase, MD 20815
(301) 961-2858
Web site: www.atv-youth.org

The 4-H ATV Safety Program helps young people, parents, caregivers, and other community members come together to help ensure that every ATV ride is a safe ride. Parents and other adults have a lot of power when they work with young people to support their safe behaviors while riding ATVs. The 4-H ATV Safety Program's Web site offers teaching/curriculum materials, including their *Leader's Guide*.

Insurance Institute for Highway Safety (IIHS)
1005 N. Glebe Rd., Ste. 800, Arlington, VA 22201
(703) 247-1500 • fax: (703) 247-1588
Web site: www.hwysafety.org

IIHS is a nonprofit research and public information organization funded by auto insurers. The institute conducts research to find effective measures to prevent motor vehicle crashes, including those that result from teen driving. On its Web site the institute publishes information on the results of its research by topic. The "Teenagers" link includes fatality statistics, articles on teen driving from the institute's newsletter *Status Report*, tables of each state's teen driving laws; and congressional testimony on issues related to teen driving.

Motorcycle Safety Foundation
(800) 446-9227
Web site: www.msf-usa.org

The Motorcycle Safety Foundation is the internationally recognized developer of the comprehensive, research-based Rider Education and Training System (MSF RETS). The RETS curriculum promotes lifelong learning for motorcyclists and continuous professional development for certified Rider Coaches and other trainers. MSF also actively participates in government relations, safety research, public awareness campaigns, and the provision of technical assistance to state training and licensing programs. Its publications include the book *MSF Guide to Motorcycling Excellence*. The MSF Web site also provides a library full of safety tips, reports, curriculum materials, and more.

National Highway Traffic Safety Administration (NHTSA)
1200 New Jersey Ave. SE, West Bldg.,Washington, DC 20590
(888) 327-4236
Web site: www.nhtsa.dot.gov

The function of NHTSA is to save lives, prevent injuries, and reduce economic costs due to traffic crashes through education, research, safety standards, and enforcement activity. NHTSA sets the motor vehicle and highway safety agenda. Its Driving Licensing Division supports states' efforts to enact improved graduated driver licensing laws and to develop training materials and procedures to reduce risk taking and improve safe decision making for these drivers. It also develops standards for driver education instructors and a standardized driver education curriculum. Its "Teen Drivers Quick Click" link provides access to facts sheets, articles, and reports on teen driving issues.

National Motorists Association (NMA)
402 W. Second St., Waunakee, WI 53597-1342
(608) 849-6000 • fax: (608) 849-8697
e-mail: nma@motorists.org
Web site: www.motorists.org

The NMA was founded to represent and protect the interests of motorists. Beyond influencing national policy, the NMA supports change from the ground up by providing resources to help individuals challenge unjust laws and tickets. The NMA Web site produces a blog called *Motorist News* and provides press releases and an online store that sells books, manuals, and more.

National Organizations for Youth Safety (NOYS)
7371 Atlas Walk Way, #109, Gainesville, VA 20155
(703) 981-0264 • fax: (703) 754-8262
e-mail: sspavone@noys.org
Website: www.noys.org

NOYS is a collaborative network of national organizations and federal agencies that serve youth and focus on youth safety and health, particularly traffic safety. On its Web site NOYS provides access to research and resources on teen driving, including "Preventing Teen Motor Crashes."

National Safety Council (NSC)
1121 Spring Lake Dr., Itasca, IL 60143-3201
(630) 285-1121 • fax: (630) 285-1315
e-mail: info@nsc.org
Web site: www.nsc.org

The NSC is a nonprofit, nongovernmental, international public service organization dedicated to protecting life and promoting health. Founded in 1913 and chartered by the U.S. Congress in 1953, the NSC's mission is to educate, protect, and influence society to adopt safety practices that prevent and mitigate human suffering and economic losses at work, in homes and communities, and on roads and highways. The NSC publishes *Safety + Health* magazine, and its Web site includes a library that provides over 162,000 documents that cover a wide range of safety issues and topics.

SADD (Students Against Destructive Decisions)
255 Main St., Marlborough, MA 01752
(877) SADD-INC • fax: (508) 481-5759
Web site: www.sadd.org

SADD's mission is to provide students with the best prevention and intervention tools possible to deal with the issues of underage drinking, other drug use, impaired driving, and other destructive decisions. SADD publishes annual reports, press releases, op-eds, and the newsletter *Decisions*. In addition, SADD produces the annual *Teens Today* project—a program that studies and reports on teens' behaviors, attitudes, and decision making about various issues.

Safe America Foundation
2480 Sandy Plains Rd., Marietta, GA 30066
(770) 973-7233
Web site: www.safeamerica.org

The mission of the Safe America Foundation is to distribute information, develop and facilitate programming, and support businesses and products with a focus on emerging health and safety issues at home and in the workplace. It also partners with civic organizations, government, and corporations to address emerging health and safety issues. It publishes on its Web site news releases such as *Safe America Happenings* and *Cyber Safety in the News*.

Teens Against Drunk Driving (TADD)
1415 W. Twenty-second St., Tower Floor, Oak Brook, IL 60523
(630) 684-2290 • fax: (630) 684-2299
e-mail: info@teensagainstdrunkdriving.org
Web site: www.teensagainstdrunkdriving.org

TADD's goal is to educate youth on the dangers of drinking and driving as well as to promote safety behind the wheel. TADD is a not-for-profit community service organization that provides high schools with a safe driving program. The program, called *Turn Onto Safe Driving*, is incorporated into a homework planner and study guide for students.

BIBLIOGRAPHY

Books

Phil Berardelli, *Safe Young Drivers: A Guide for Parents and Teens.* Vienna, VA: Nautilus Communications, 2006.

Steve Casper, *ATVs: Everything You Need to Know.* Osceola, WI: Motorbooks, 2006.

Consumers Union of U.S., *Consumer Reports New Car Buying Guide 2008.* Yonkers, NY: Consumers Union of U.S., 2008.

Karen Gravelle, *The Driving Book: Everything New Drivers Need to Know but Don't Know to Ask.* New York: Walker, 2005.

Pat Hahn, *How to Ride a Motorcycle: A Rider's Guide to Strategy, Safety and Skill Development.* Osceola, WI: Motorbooks, 2005.

James Joseph, *110 Car and Driving Emergencies and How to Survive Them: The Complete Guide to Staying Safe on the Road.* Guilford, CT: Lyons, 2003.

John H. Loughry, *Saving Our Teen Drivers: Using Aviation Safety Skills on the Roadways.* Ashland, OH: Seminee, 2005.

Michael Schein, *Teenage Roadhogs.* 2nd ed. Charleston, SC: BookSurge, 2006.

Anthony Scotti, *Professional Driving Techniques: The Essential Guide to Operating a Motor Vehicle with Confidence and Skill.* Ormond Beach, FL: PhotoGraphics, 2007.

Timothy C. Smith, *Crashproof Your Kids: Make Your Teen a Safer, Smarter Driver.* Forest City, NC: Fireside, 2006.

Periodicals

Daniel Albalate, "Lowering Blood Alcohol Content Levels to Save Lives: The European Experience," *Journal of Policy Analysis and Management,* Winter 2008.

Jennifer Axelbanda, Christopher Stromskia, Nathaniel McQuay Jr., and Michael Heller, "Are All-Terrain Vehicle Injuries

Becoming More Severe?" *Accident Analysis & Prevention*, March 2007.

J.F. Bowman, Michele Fields, Tom Rice, and Arlene Greenspan, "Children, Teens, Motor Vehicles and the Law," *Journal of Law, Medicine & Ethics*, Winter 2007.

Christopher Carpenter, "Did Ontario's Zero Tolerance & Graduated Licensing Law Reduce Youth Drunk Driving?" *Journal of Policy Analysis and Management*, Winter 2006.

Rob Decker, "Crash Testing in the Lab: Putting a New Stop to the CO_2 Car!" *Tech Directions*, October 2005.

Amy Dickinson, "Riding in Cars with Girls: When It Comes to Unsafe Driving, Girls Are Reaching Parity with Boys," *Time*, January 21, 2002.

David C. Grabowski and Michael A. Morrisey, "Graduated Driver Licensing and Teen Traffic Fatalities," *Journal of Health Economics*, May 2005.

James Hedlund, "Novice Teen Driving: GDL and Beyond," *Journal of Safety Research*, no. 2, 2007.

Ed Henry, "Risky Business: At This School, Teen Drivers Get into Trouble to Learn How to Avoid It on the Road," *Kiplinger's*, September 2002.

John Lee, "Technology and Teen Drivers," *Journal of Safety Research*, no. 2, 2007.

Anne T. McCartta, Laurie A. Hellingaa, and Emily R. Haireb, "Age of Licensure and Monitoring Teenagers' Driving: Survey of Parents of Novice Teenage Drivers," *Journal of Safety Research*, no. 6, 2007.

Michael A. Morrisey and David C. Grabowski, "Graduated Drivers License Programs and Rural Teenage Motor Vehicle Fatalities," *Journal of Rural Health*, Fall 2006.

Matt Sundeen, "Driving While Distracted: Inexperienced Teen Drivers Too Often Take Fatal Risks," *State Legislatures*, May 2008.

Christopher Welsh, "Harry Potter and the Underage Drinkers: Can We Use This to Talk to Teens About Alcohol?" *Journal of Child & Adolescent Substance Abuse*, July 2007.

Allan F. Williams, "Contribution of the Components of Graduated Licensing to Crash Reductions," *Journal of Safety Research*, no. 2, 2007.

Kenneth L. Zuber, "Death at the Wheel: Traditional Driver Education Does Little to Educate New Drivers," *Auto Week*, September 4, 2006.

PICTURE CREDITS